PRIVATE CASE–
PUBLIC SCANDAL

PRIVATE CASE —
PUBLIC SCANDAL

PETER FRYER

LONDON
SECKER & WARBURG

First published in England 1966 by
Martin Secker & Warburg Limited
14 Carlisle Street, London W1

Copyright © Peter Fryer 1966

Printed in Great Britain by
Western Printing Services Ltd, Bristol

TO MY FRIENDS AT THE BRITISH MUSEUM

'I want a poor student to have the same means of indulging his learned curiosity, of following his rational pursuits, of consulting the same authorities, of fathoming the most intricate inquiry, as the richest man in the kingdom, as far as books go, and I contend that Government is bound to give him the most liberal and unlimited assistance in this respect.'

Sir Anthony Panizzi (1797–1879), principal librarian of the British Museum, 1856–66

'We are keepers of books, not guardians of morals.'

Sir Frank Francis (b. 1901), director and principal librarian of the British Museum since 1959, as quoted in *The Sunday Times*, January 6, 1963

CONTENTS

CONTENTS

INTRODUCTION

In 1962 the trustees of the British Museum published, after 203 years, the first comprehensive guide to the public services offered by that institution. In seventy-two pages this booklet told the seeker after knowledge how to find the lantern slides, Anglo-Saxon coins, Egyptian and Greek papyri, Japanese woodcuts, or other treasures he needed to see. He was told about guide lectures, and how to obtain photographs of objects in the collections. He was told the conditions under which he might sketch with pencil, crayon, or fountain-pen in the exhibition galleries, and how to obtain a ticket for the reading room ('The Trustees', he was warned, 'cannot accept the recommendations of hotel or boarding-house keepers in favour of their guests'). He was even provided with a list of the three nearest Underground stations and the numbers of the twenty-six nearest bus routes.

All this, and much more, was an attempt to answer the complaint that the British Museum did not make its services well enough or widely enough known; at all events, that was how Sir Frank Francis, K.C.B., director and principal librarian, put it in his introductory note. Sir Frank had a word of apology for the students' rooms, and the reading rooms in the library departments, not being 'as well designed or as well co-ordinated as we should like'. On the other hand, there were picture postcards and Christmas cards to be proud of and, had he been writing in 1966, he might well have added a word about the museum's delightful pictorial calendars. With no less pride, Sir Frank summed up the standard of public service which is supposed to inform the entire work of the museum, including its library of about eight million volumes:

> Universality of material involves the application of universality of use: every kind of service to every kind of person. The collections have been organised with this obligation in view and they are available, *in toto*, to the public whether in the exhibition galleries or in the students' rooms. Here the student, however advanced or however humble, can rely on finding material he needs from moment to moment; he can check his references. . . .
>
> The catalogues prepared by the various Departments of the Museum have always been famous for their range and their scholarship. They are supported by specialised monographs . . . on subjects represented in the collections. . . .
>
> The services of the expert staff are always available for genuine enquirers and . . . we are doing our best to provide good conditions under which the collections can be viewed and studied.

The innocent reader of this booklet, as he glanced at the picture facing page 33, could have had no inkling that the photographer was standing hard by a collection of books which have never been available *in toto* to the public; a collection in which no student, least of all a 'humble' one, can ever 'rely' on finding the material he needs, even when it is there; a collection in which the checking of references is attended with endless difficulties and frustrations; a collection which, by decision of the trustees, found no place at that time in the general catalogue and is not even now, and is not to be, represented in the subject indexes based on the general catalogue. The caption to the picture in question reads: 'The Arch Room housing incunabula.' Incunabula, to bibliographers, are books printed before 1500 and the arch room, to which only members of the staff are admitted, does house a great many such books, no doubt in ideal conditions of temperature and humidity. It also houses about five thousand erotic and sexological works in English, French, Italian, Spanish, Portuguese, German, Dutch, and Latin, including what might be called the cream of the world's pornography.

So far as I am able to judge, the Ministry of Works photographer must have positioned his camera pretty closely to the locked press known as 'P.C. 25', where *The Confessional Unmasked* (1851) rubs joints, as it were, with *Ten Tales from the islands of Alu, Mono, Fauru* (Leipzig, 1912–13) by Gerald Camden Wheeler, and where *Human Gorillas: a study of rape with violence* (Paris, 1901) by 'Count Roscaud' squeezes up against the original French edition (1883) of *Padlocks and Girdles of Chastity* (Paris, 1892) by Alcide Bonneau (1836–1904). The picture shows, in the next bay along, a jacket thrown nonchalantly over the back of a chair by some ardent labourer in this vineyard, and behind it are visible one empty press and about half of a second. The first of these presses, which I fancy is now numbered 'P.C. 13', is being filled, as cataloguing proceeds, by the magnificent Dawes collection, willed to the British Museum by this country's last great collector of erotica, the late Charles Reginald Dawes. The exotic fruits, superbly bound, of Dawes's lifelong devotion to his hobby were carried reverently into the museum at six o'clock one summer morning of 1964 by officials who had made an overnight journey to Gotherington in Gloucestershire. Their pleasure in their valuable acquisitions was noticeably diminished when, on checking through them, they found no trace of two of the choicest items: *Suburban Souls: the erotic psychology of a man and a maid* (Paris, 1901) and *The Memoirs of a Voluptuary: the secret life of an English boarding-school* ('New Orleans' [i.e. Paris], 1905), the latter described by Dawes himself as 'what, after due consideration, I deem to be the best of all English erotic books, after *Fanny Hill*' and as 'a model of what a frankly erotic work should be ... interesting, amusing, vivid and well written'.

If, as I imagine, the half-visible empty press in the photograph is now 'P.C. 14', it is partly filled with the collection of a friend of the late Stephen Ward. He is said to have decided, some time during the Profumo affair, that his collection of erotica might cause him some embarrassment if police discovered them on his premises. The British Museum officials accepted his gift with mixed feelings, which they expressed, not uncharacteristically, by retaining the Olympia Press publications and other printed matter and passing on the semi-literate 'Soho typescripts' to the Institute for Sex Research at Bloomington, Indiana, familiarly known as the Kinsey Institute. The part of the collection which stayed at Bloomsbury filled many gaps: the student of late Victorian music-hall can now round out his knowledge with at any rate the first volume of *Crissie* (1899); and the reader of Mr Christopher Logue and Mr Alexander Trocchi can, if he is persistent enough, gain access to some of their less celebrated juvenilia.

It is not untypical, again, of the department of printed books that the arch room is described in the caption as housing only incunabula when, throughout the entire department, its principal claim to fame is that it houses erotica. But to advertise this fact in a guide to public services would have been to violate one of the museum's strongest taboos. The BM collection of erotica is without doubt the most comprehensive in the world. The Kinsey collection, at any rate so far as the classics and other older examples of this genre are concerned, does not hold a candle to it. The celebrated *Enfer* of the *Bibliothèque nationale* in Paris probably runs it a close second; but the alleged riches, in this field, possessed by the Vatican, the Library of Congress, and the Bodleian in Oxford, turn out to be small fry indeed compared with Bloomsbury's well-stocked private case. There is this difference however: these other great libraries have always been courageous enough, and honest enough, and scholarly enough, to include their entire erotic and sexological collections in their main catalogues; only recently, and only after some of us had kicked up a fuss, was the decision taken by the trustees of the BM to begin incorporating the private case collection in the general catalogue. At the time when the guide to the museum's public services was published, in 1962, not a word was ever said to readers, either orally or in any printed or duplicated guide, to suggest that the library possessed a good many important books which were not to be found in the general catalogue—unless a reader happened to ask about a particular book and was persistent. And even then he might be told, in error, that the BM did not have a copy when in fact it had. This has been my experience several times.

The nearest approach to guidance was a vague reference,

in a leaflet for new readers, to 'certain other classes of books' which, in addition to named categories of rare books, were 'normally seen in the North Library'. No hint of the deficiency of the general catalogue was to be found in Sir Frank Francis's standard paper on the BM catalogues and subject indexes, first published in the June 1948 issue of the *Journal of Documentation* and twice reprinted. However eminent the scholar, he was left in ignorance of the very existence of a private case unless he was preternaturally suspicious. So that, for instance, Professor Vivian de Sola Pinto and Dr Allan Edwin Rodway, in *The Common Muse: an anthology of popular British ballad poetry* (1957), whilst acknowledging the 'courteous assistance' given them by the BM officials, make it clear that they are quite unaware of any unexpurgated edition of *The Merry Muses of Caledonia* by Robert Burns and others being in the museum. Indeed, they thank Dr David Daiches for the loan of his copy of the 'otherwise unobtainable' *Merry Muses*. These students, advanced though they were, did not find the book they needed in the BM precisely because the catalogue they were relying on was deficient in range and scholarship, while there was no specialized monograph which might have compensated for its deficiencies, and the courteous assistance of the expert staff did not extend to dropping the smallest hint to these genuine inquirers that the museum possessed, locked away and uncatalogued, not one but *ten* copies of various editions of the very book they sought! The open republication of *The Merry Muses* recently has resulted in all ten copies being transferred from the private case to the general library.

Sir Frank Francis was editor of *The Library* from 1936 to 1953, lecturer in bibliography at the School of Librarianship of University College, London, from 1945 to 1959, and vice-president of the Unesco International Advisory Committee on Bibliography from 1954 to 1960. Since 1947 he has been on the editorial board of the *Journal of Documentation*. He is supposed to have been the prime mover in the trustees' recent decision to enter the titles of private case books in the general catalogue. It is greatly to his credit if he was.

While this book was in the press, it was announced that Mr R. A. Wilson, whose statements are frequently quoted in these pages, is retiring this September from the post of principal keeper of printed books. His successor is said to have it in mind to liberalize BM policy towards erotica. Half the books at present in the private case are, I am informed, to be removed from that category. Changes of this kind, for which a few of us have been agitating for several years, will be most welcome and will prove how right we have been to agitate.

I

BEHIND THE CUPBOARD DOOR

It is now five years since I became aware that the British Museum possesses 'special' books, and special rules for them. In those days I had not the good fortune to be a regular—i.e. a daily—reader. Two evenings a week and Saturdays were the most I could normally manage, since I had not yet emancipated myself from the need to work elsewhere for a living. Consequently I was not so well known to the officials as is now, perhaps, the case. There came a week when I had occasion to consult two books on sexual questions: a work by William Acton called *The Functions and Disorders of the Reproductive Organs in Youth, in Adult Age, and in Advanced Life* and Iwan Bloch's *Sexual Life in England Past and Present*.

William Acton (1813–75) was the second son of a clergyman and became an authority on venereal diseases and prostitution. He wrote *Prostitution Considered in its Moral, Social, and Sanitary Aspects, in London and Other Large Cities* (1857). His *Functions and Disorders* first appeared as a separate monograph in 1857, with appendices on masturbation and on the copulative act in the bee. The sixth edition came out in the year of its author's death, by which time the first appendix had swollen into a whole section, with such chapter titles as 'Insanity arising from Masturbation'. My chief purpose in consulting Acton was to discover in what context he had called it a 'vile aspersion' on women to suggest that they experienced sexual pleasure. This is one of those standbys of popular sexology which get copied from writer to writer because they are such a bother to check. Exceptionally, I found the original context even more revealing than the somewhat misleading stock quotation. Here is what Acton wrote, in the third edition (1862) of *Functions and Disorders*:

> The majority of women (happily for them*) are not very much troubled with sexual feeling of any kind. . . . Married men . . . or married women . . . would vindicate female nature from the vile aspersions cast on it by the abandoned conduct and ungoverned lusts of a few of its worst examples. . . . The best mothers, wives, and managers of households, know little or nothing of sexual indulgences. . . . As a general rule, a modest woman seldom desires any sexual gratification for herself. She submits to her husband, but only to please him; and, but for the desire of maternity, would far rather be relieved from his attentions.

In another passage, scarcely less memorable, hard-working London intellectuals are advised not to copulate more frequently than once every seven to ten days.

So much for Acton. Iwan Bloch (1872–1922) was the author of a number of sexological works which rely rather heavily on secondary authorities and show a touching inability to discriminate between pornographers' fantasies and historical fact. One of these works, *Das Geschlechtsleben in England* (Charlottenburg-Berlin, 1901–03), pub-

* In the fifth edition (1871) this was changed to: 'happily for society'.

lished under the pseudonym 'Dr. Eugen Dühren', appeared in at least two and a half abridged English editions in the nineteen-thirties, and has had the compliment paid it of being plundered by virtually every popular sexologist who has put pen to paper over the past three decades. Without adequate acknowledgement, for the most part. Almost always the English version is used, in which quotations from English writers are retranslated from the German without any attempt having been made to check them against the originals. The results are often misleading and sometimes ludicrous. It was certain of these quotations I wanted to examine.

There appeared on my desk in the reading room a small pile of grubby, well-thumbed editions of Acton—and my application slip for Bloch, marked 'please see superintendent'.

That gentleman was as courteous as most of the museum officials are, leaving aside one notable exception of each sex. He had to satisfy himself, he said, that my purpose in applying for Bloch's book was serious and that I was unlikely to steal, mark, or mutilate it. Was I engaged on serious research? Was I perhaps writing something which made it necessary to see this work?

It was a brief examination, conducted in a manner to which no one with honest intentions could have objected, though I could not help feeling that mere possession of a ticket of admission to the reading room, for which, after all, one needs a recommendation from some respectable person (and not an hotel or boarding-house keeper), ought to establish the reader's bona fides. It has since been put to me that the intention of this kind of interview is to protect books from readers, which experience shows to be a necessary part of a librarian's duty, rather than to protect readers from books, which is not thought to be a librarian's business in this country. Such a distinction did not emerge quite so clearly in the course of the interview and, despite the superintendent's civil manner, I did not see that my reasons for wanting to read Bloch were anything to do with him. I wondered what he would have said if I had told him I wanted to read the book for pleasure, or from idle curiosity, or to enrich my fantasies. The answer, I now suppose, to any reader mischievous or honest enough to give such a reason would be that the BM does not cater for readers in search of pleasure—other than the epiphenomenal pleasure engendered by a piece of serious research industriously carried out.

My application slip in due course came back a second time, now bearing the information that the book I wished to see was available in the north library. This is a reading room for those who want to consult rare and otherwise valuable books. They are divided into two factions: those who want the windows open and those who want them shut. In hot weather and cold, the attendants dispense justice like so many Solomons, and the defeated faction sulks in its overcoats or shirtsleeves, as the case may be. I was asked to sit at the table immediately under the eyes of the attendants as they stood at their counter dispensing justice and rare books; and there, for several hours, I sat and read Iwan Bloch's *Sexual Life in England Past and Present*— the 1938 edition, limited to one thousand copies.

I hope I have made it clear that I was not, even then, oblivious of the need to protect books from thieves, mutilators, and scribblers; though I did not yet realize how great a problem these persons present to the authorities of our national library. It seemed to me that there was little to choose, from the point of view of sexual frankness, between

Acton and Bloch. Here, to my mind, was an anomaly. If the contents of a sexological work were the criterion, and Bloch was protected, why not also Acton? Conversely, if Acton could be read freely by dirty-fingered and, perhaps, dirty-minded readers in the reading room, why not Bloch? If the museum authorities chose to exercise some kind of censorship, for very respectable reasons no doubt, why was it not consistent, impartial, all-embracing?

This was the burden of the letter I wrote to the superintendent of the reading room. The reply came from a more exalted official, the keeper in charge of public services, to whom the superintendent is responsible and through whom he submits, to the still more exalted principal keeper of printed books, an annual report each April Fool's Day. The reply boiled down to this: illustrated works had been found more attractive to thieves, mutilators, and scribblers than those without illustrations. Bloch was illustrated, Acton was not.

The 1938 edition of Bloch is indeed illustrated. It has a frontispiece and thirty-one plates, mostly by those vigorous immortalizers of English low life, Rowlandson, Hogarth, and Gillray (who appears in the list of illustrations as Gilroy). These plates depict ladies in dishabille; buxom ladies being clasped by randy soldiers; callipygian ladies being fondled by grotesque men; wenches having their bottoms pinched; gross, gouty, old fellows having their chins tickled by pretty young girls; a painter and his naked model disturbed by leering intruders; strolling players dressing and undressing; a drunken orgy at the mansion of a duke of York; a young man stealing the clothes of two bathing damsels; more naked bathers in the Thames, watched by an avid, elderly prude; 'A Boarding-School-Miss taking an Evening Lesson! !'; and a pious gentleman

20

paralysed between the delights of gluttony and fornication as effectively as Buridan's ass half-way between two identical bales of hay. Drawings as coarse or coarser, drawings far more titillating, far fuller of innuendo—though none, I think, so pungent as social comment—are to be seen today wherever there is a display of paperbacks. Whoever wishes to possess an erotic drawing by Rowlandson, Hogarth, or Gillray is going to excessively complicated and risky lengths if he wields his razor blade in the north library. In 1966 terms, the result in comic pictures simply isn't worth the trouble or the risk.

Nevertheless I cannot pretend that the museum authorities are wrong to protect, by close supervision of their use, whatever books their experience suggests are in need of such protection. Sometimes their choice of what to protect and what to leave unprotected appears anomalous, or a bit daft. But the responsibility is theirs, after all, and it is probably better that the net should be cast a little too widely than that there should be more books stolen, more illustrations of female genitalia removed, more anti-sexual annotations by religious fanatics in the margins. The problem is a real one. Some people are kinky about such books. They cannot help themselves. Their fingers itch for a pencil, or a sharp knife, or the thrill of possession. It is annoying to find a book you want to read has been stolen, or slashed, or—as a friend of mine found—enriched with a used condom, which is not so agreeable a discovery as a pressed flower in a seventeenth-century herbal.

Books protected in the way Bloch's *Sexual Life in England* is protected—i.e. the superintendent must sign the application, the book must be read at the 'front bench' in the north library, but there *is* an entry in the general catalogue—are known in museum jargon as 'cupboard books'.

21

Whether or not they are actually kept in a cupboard, as one lady writer on these topics suggested recently, seems to me of purely academic interest. They could be kept in a tea-chest for all I care, so long as readers who want them have access to them, complete, unexpurgated, unmutilated. You can spot these books in the general catalogue by their pressmarks, which always begin Cup. 363 to 367 or Cup. 800 to 804. The former are sexological works, books on contraception, guides to erotic technique and coital postures, sociological surveys of teenage copulation in Cockfosters and homosexuality in Rutland. Under this rubric you will find the Kinsey volumes and many of the works of Havelock Ellis, Marie Stopes, Magnus Hirschfeld, Richard von Krafft-Ebing, and Norman Haire, together with sundry writings by popularizers, imitators, and epigones. If Cup. 363 to 367 gives us sexual science, Cup. 800 to 804 gives us erotic art: nudist and girly magazines, 'art studies', books on the cinema containing pictures of women in provocative poses, learned works on strip-tease (in French) with similar illustrations. . . . Some of these publications—those whose only apparent function is to supplement the masturbation fantasies of lonely and unimaginative men—might be thought scarcely worth protecting. Even the Kinsey Institute, I understand, bothers to collect only one issue per year of each of the cheesecake type of periodical. But the copies the BM receives under the Copyright Act will no doubt be of some interest and value to future social historians, who will probably prefer not to have them slashed to ribbons. It is not for the present generation to choose what to save and what to discard.

Then there are the Cup. 1000 and Cup. 1001 pressmarks, which will be explained later, and various other cupboard pressmarks for which no superintendent's signature is needed:

Cup. 400 and Cup. 500, which are irrelevant to our theme, and Cup. 700, which seems to embrace books on sexual questions, or with piquant illustrations, which north library readers can be trusted to use elsewhere than at the 'front bench'. A book of my own has this pressmark, and when I applied for it while writing the present book I *was* asked to see the superintendent. I thought my leg was being pulled, but it turned out that a new member of the staff had made a mistake. Less recent Cup. 700 items are runs of *Lilliput* and *London Life*, two names still with power to arouse nostalgia in men over forty. *Lilliput*, the younger generation may like to know, brightened the second world war for soldiers and schoolboys with pin-ups and some intelligent letterpress; the many copies stolen from the BM set are still brightening someone's private library, no doubt. *London Life*, in the thirties, was the most comprehensive and lively fetichists' journal this country has ever seen. Its correspondents exchanged experiences and fantasies —impossible to distinguish—on everything from wooden legs to tight lacing and from eleven-inch heels to rubber undergarments. Early in the war it changed hands and character, and a valuable source of data on a good many harmless pastimes dried up. I should perhaps emphasize that the recently founded magazine of the same name has no resemblance whatever to its long-defunct and, by all serious students, regretted namesake. I wish it were possible to say that the old *London Life* is all there, at Bloomsbury; but here is another case where protection is too little and too late. The BM run of the old *London Life* used to be kept at the newspaper repository, where it suffered greatly from the over-keen razor blades of some of the serious students who made the pilgrimage to Colindale to consult it.

I have never been able to find out who decides whether

a given book needs protection and, if so, how exactly it is to be classified. Perhaps it is the cataloguing division; or perhaps those mysterious and powerful backroom men and women, surely the grey eminences of the BM, known as 'placers'. Theirs is the responsibility for seeing that a book receives an appropriate pressmark and gets safely into the right press and on the right shelf. There is no mystery about the decision as to who may or may not see Cup. 363 and Cup. 800 books. This depends on the superintendent of the reading room or his deputy. The criteria on which the decision is supposed to be based are far from clear, however.

There is in existence a duplicated document called *Information for those Superintending in the Reading Room*, which was circulated to certain members of the staff in March 1966 and a copy of which was procured for me by a friend who knew of my interest in library administration. This document lists the contents of the drawers in the superintendent's desk, including his reading glass (for loan to readers) and rubber stamps (not for loan), and gives all kinds of details about his keys, his 'in' and 'out' and other trays, his thermometer, and various mysterious instruments in his possession 'intended to control the heat and humidity' of the reading room. But the document grows suddenly and unaccountably vague under the heading: 'Cupboard Books, Novels Published within the Last Five Years, etc.' It says merely: 'If the superintendent is satisfied of the need to do so, he authorizes the issue of cupboard books, novels, etc.' I am not aware that serious inquirers ever have much difficulty in obtaining permission to see cupboard books (though one female deputy superintendent assumes a glacial manner when asked, no matter how politely, to perform this part of her duties). But would an unknown reader in, say, a dirty mackintosh, tieless and

24

suffering from a facial tic and a Cockney accent, satisfy a deputy superintendent quite so easily as a reader outwardly more 'respectable'? It seems at least arguable that the protection afforded by the 'special table' in the north library ought to be enough, without this preliminary interview. Especially now that Lady Snow has taken it upon herself to send to the British Museum reading room those requiring information on sexual pathology.

It has been suggested to me by members of the staff that the talk with the superintendent is meant merely to discourage 'frivolous' applications on the part of sensation-seekers easily put off by the prospect of an embarrassing interview. I am not disposed to share the view that sensation-seekers are so easily discouraged. But if this is in fact its purpose, then the interview should be abolished, since those who most need instruction in sexual matters—the young, the shy, the misfits, the impotent, the maladjusted—are precisely those who might shrink from justifying to an official, however courteous, their need to see such and such a book on sex. There is enough ignorance on sexual questions and consequent unhappiness without the BM authorities' adding to it through what is in practice, even if not in intention, a form of censorship. It may be said that it is not the museum's function to provide for the sexual enlightenment of individuals not engaged in serious research. But who is to draw the line between the occupational needs of the genuine researcher and the contingent needs of the merely curious? Marie Stopes, when her first marriage had not been consummated after six months, sought enlightenment in the British Museum library. This was long before she emerged as a writer on sex and birth control. Her reading enabled her to sue successfully as *virgo intacta* for the annulment of the marriage. Would it seriously be suggested that her

researches constituted an improper use of the library's resources? And, if it was all right for an obscure lady palaeo-
botanist to use the BM for so private a purpose before the
first world war, why is it not all right for any ticket-holder to
do the same today? Provided the books are protected while
in use, by discreet but adequate invigilation, no attempt
should be made to frighten off any inquirer; sexological
works should be available without formality to all who
apply for them. It is books which need protection, from
certain readers; however much certain readers may need
protection from books, it is no part of the BM officials' job
to provide it.

II

DISCOVERY OF A TABOO

PROTECTING BOOKS by making sure readers handle them properly is one thing. Protecting books, or readers, or the good name of the British Museum, by keeping titles out of the general catalogue and subject indexes is quite another. Like most readers who discover that these aids to research are imperfect because censored, I stumbled on their imperfections by accident and could not, for some time, reconcile this discovery with the idealized view I held of the BM as a stronghold of liberalism and enlightenment. The BM seemed to embody certain liberal values: democracy, for instance, in that all readers were, on the whole, treated alike; freedom, in that no obstacle was put in the way of serious inquiry in any field. I thought of it as an institution which, whatever the régime in power, would ignore a government instruction to remove, as it were, an encyclopaedia article on Beria and substitute one on the Bering Strait.

The BM has indeed much to offer of which trustees, officials, staff, and public alike can be proud. In particular, the library provides without charge an unlimited number of books to any one reader on any one day. For some of its readers it is their university, and many of them have a great deal of affection for it. One hears criticisms now and again about the high cost of Xerox copies and the lack of locker facilities for readers. The tea-room was recently the subject of reasonable strictures by Mr Eric Lubbock, M.P. Less justified criticisms are heard occasionally from new readers about the length of time it takes to receive a book after applying for it—between thirty minutes and an hour.* These critics judge a great library containing millions of volumes on miles of shelves by the standards of a municipal lending library. The service is in fact reasonably good, though strained more and more each summer by the growing number of foreign scholars and young women from Italy who use the reading room. The staff are generally helpful and courteous, even when readers are rude, or stupid, or both. A week at the *Bibliothèque nationale*, one often feels, would be an eye-opener for some of these critics.

I have myself received many kindnesses at the hands of officials and staff, and I should not wish the hard things said in this book about certain aspects of British Museum policy and practice to be construed as blanket criticism or ingratitude. None of the staff, and not all the officials, are responsible for the imperfections of which this book complains. Many of them, I dare say, would be greatly relieved if those imperfections were removed. But there are some officials who would doubtless feel affronted if judged as librarians or scholars. Their allegiance is not to science, whether bibliographical, historical, or sexological. They are civil servants. However much it might sadden them to be told, by some latter-day Savonarola, to 'burn the vanities' in their possession, they would obey. As it is, though

* If however you are baron Chuter-Ede or the archbishop of Canterbury, you do not have to wait longer than twenty minutes, even when you have only the title of the book you want to see and not the author's name. Cf. *Parliamentary Debates: Standing Committee A: British Museum Bill*, March 5, 1963, col. 42–3.

28

they are not rewriting history in the Russian fashion, they are burying part of the historian's sources—without marking the grave.

Soon after my reading of Acton and Bloch, I came across an article on tabooed words by the American philologist Allen Walker Read, in which he mentioned two works I had never heard of. One was called Κρυπτάδια (pronounced 'Kruptadia' and meaning 'Hidden Things' or 'Secret Things'), with a subtitle in French describing it as a 'Collection of documents for use in the study of popular traditions'. The other was called *The Slang of Venery*. I could find neither in the general catalogue.

At that time the reading room had a suggestions book, now replaced by separate cards not available for inspection by other readers until they have been commented on by the acquisitions or Slavonic divisions; somehow this is less fun than the book used to be, perhaps because readers can no longer comment on each other's suggestions or use the book for complaints, in verse. When I put Κρυπτάδια and *The Slang of Venery* in the book a note appeared, in due course, advising me to see the reading-room superintendent. And so, one evening, I addressed myself to the deputy superintendent on duty. After telling me what Κρυπτάδια meant, which was not what I was asking him, he revealed somewhat reluctantly that the library had a number of books whose titles were deliberately omitted from the catalogue. He went away to look up the two I had asked about, in a private catalogue inaccessible to readers, and came back with the information that the BM had a copy of *The Slang of Venery* but no copy of Κρυπτάδια. He could not however give me the former's pressmark, since to do so would be a breach of the Official Secrets Act. This was said unsmilingly, and it did not occur to me that he might be joking. How could I consult this uncatalogued book? I must write, he said, to the principal keeper of printed books, Mr R. A. Wilson, c.b., requesting permission to see it and stating my reasons.

I wrote such a letter there and then, and handed it in. Next day, remembering a casual glance some years before, I visited the London Library and took from its open shelves, in the section labelled 'Bibliography: Prohibited Books',* the *Registrum librorum eroticorum* (1936) of a compiler calling himself 'Rolf S. Reade'. This was the anagrammatic pseudonym of Alfred Rose, a well-known London bookman of the twenties and early thirties. His *Registrum*, a list of over five thousand erotic and sexological books, was arranged for publication after his death by a bookseller called W. J. Stanislas, who made a pretty poor job of it. There is a mistake of one sort or another in well over half its 5,061 entries. For all that, it does provide the only accessible key to the BM private case, since Rose, by some rare dispensation on the part of the principal keeper of the day, had the privilege of seeing the private case catalogue and was even allowed to copy it out, in a dim light. To the titles thus gleaned he added others transcribed from the catalogues of the Bodleian, Cambridge university library, the Guildhall library (the Edward Phelips collection of erotica, transferred to the BM private case in 1950), the *Bibliothèque nationale*, and the Vatican—as well as the contents, unidentified as such but unmistakable, of the Dawes collection. Most important of all, the BM private case titles each had its appropriate pressmark, though some are not

* It has since been removed to the safety of the librarian's room and locked up, after standing on the open shelves, unmutilated and unstolen, for twenty-eight years.

quite correct and others have since been changed. Here, then, is a summary, and a useful one, of the contents of the private case in 1935 or so. And here, without undue difficulty, I found an entry for Κρυπτάδια, complete with BM pressmark.

My next step was to write once more to the principal keeper, asking to see this work too, and citing the pressmark given by Rose. I also quoted the deputy superintendent's words about the Official Secrets Act and asked if he were not perhaps misinformed, since private case pressmarks were so readily accessible in the *Registrum*.

The principal keeper replied that he could not explain why I had been told Κρυπτάδια was not in the library. His letter went on:

> The rule that readers may not consult the Private Case catalogue is of long standing and is designed to put a check on what I might perhaps call indiscriminate browsing in the field of erotica. It is quite true that the publication of Reade's *Registrum* has greatly weakened the force of this regulation but there have been a good many accessions since the publication of that work and, subject to a new direction from higher authority, I propose to continue to enforce it. Moreover, it is precisely in order to prevent the publication of another work similar to that of Reade that we normally do not disclose the pressmarks of Private Case books.
>
> I hope that these regulations do not seem to you unduly onerous. We certainly do not wish to hinder serious research, still less to act as censors, but it is my view that we are under an obligation to limit the use of these works to serious researchers.

I gather that the reference to the Official Secrets Act was intended rather light-heartedly. I have told the official in question to choose his words more carefully in future.

One long-term result of this exchange was that 'the official in question' has looked upon me with a jaundiced eye ever since. If he should happen to read these lines, I hope he will accept my assurance that my question about the Official Secrets Act was a straightforward request for information and not an attempt to have him carpeted, and that I am sorry for any *ennuis* my imperfect sense of humour may have caused him.

The short-term result of the exchange was that I could examine, after a nine days' delay, both Κρυπτάδια and *The Slang of Venery*.

The first of these works consists of twelve dumpy polyglot volumes, bound in red. Four of them were published at Heilbronn, a town a few miles north of Stuttgart, between the years 1883 and 1888; the remainder were published in Paris from 1898 to 1911. The series was edited anonymously by three eminent scholars: the Polish anthropologist Izydor Kopernicki (1827–91); Friedrich Saloman Krauss (b. 1859), who also edited the similar series *Anthropophyteía* (1904–13) and two supplementary series; and the philologist Gaston Paris (1839–1903). These three could not put their names to their work in this field during their lifetimes because the material they printed, at first in 210 and later in only 175 copies, was in those days regarded as altogether foul, so foul as to be beneath scientific notice. Κρυπτάδια is in fact the first scientific collection of erotic and scatological folklore: tales from Russia, Bulgaria, France, Belgium, Spain, and Italy; erotic riddles from

Britanny; customs and beliefs recorded in Scotland; lavatory wall epigraphy from France; French erotic songs, complete with music; jokes from many countries; and sexual vocabularies, including a rather skimpy extract from Francis Grose's *Classical Dictionary of the Vulgar Tongue* (1785). It is a sad commentary on BM censorship that many pages of the BM copy of such a rich collection are uncut to this day, so effectively has it been concealed from folklorists since the museum began to acquire it over eighty years ago.

There is not much from England in it, but at least one of the learned contributors seems to have had a special interest in Wales, supplying a lengthy 'Welsh Ædœology', or essay on Welsh erotic and scatological vocabulary, and the text and an English translation of 'A Welshman's Lament' by Lewis, son of Edward. The last verse of this early seventeenth-century complaint about a clap contracted by a Welsh visitor to London promises that

> If I ever get well of the pain I have got
>   To my bitter woe,
>   I will never again on account of the pain
>   Enter a lady's drawers without a spare prick.

Students of Celtic languages and literature who wish to consult the original will find it in the BM's department of manuscripts (Add. MS. 14964). Κρυπτάδια's ninth volume, published in 1905, contains a defective version of *Sodom*, a highly obscene play almost certainly written by 'the Great, the God-like *Rochester*', as Aphra Behn called him, about the year 1668 and printed, probably in London but with the false imprint 'Antwerp', in 1684. No copy of this edition is known to exist, and the play has come down to us in seven imperfect manuscripts, one of which is also in the

BM (Harl. MS. 7312). Subtitled 'The Quintessence of Debauchery', and 'Written for the Royall Company of Whoremasters', *Sodom* was a satire on the homosexual court of king James I. The king of Sodom is called Bolloxinion; his queen, Cuntigratia; their children, Pricket and Swivia; the general of the king's army, Buggeranthos; and the queen's maids of honour, Fuckadilla, Officina, Cunticula, and Clitoris. Virtuoso is the name of the merkin- and dildo-maker to the royal family, though despite his name his wares do not go uncriticized. The play's theme is an unsuccessful attempt by the king to impose homosexuality in place of heterosexuality. Besides the Κρυπτάδια edition of *Sodom*, the BM's private case also has a German translation, privately printed in Leipzig and dated 1909, adorned with grotesque phallic drawings by Julius Klinger, somewhat in the style of Aubrey Beardsley.

The Slang of Venery, duplicated and published privately in 1916 by a Chicago newspaperman called Henry N. Cary, is essentially a reprint of the relevant articles in the seven-volume *Slang and its Analogues* (1890–1904) by the mysterious John Stephen Farmer and his poet friend William Ernest ('captain of my soul') Henley. To these articles is added material taken from earlier dictionaries of English slang and cant, of which there have been a good many. *The Slang of Venery* is thus an unoriginal but moderately useful amalgam of earlier sources, though it exasperatingly confuses sexual slang with sexual metaphor and is swollen with a large number of irrelevant periphrastic quotations from *Fanny Hill*. There are notes of varying interest and utility on appliances—including bidet, condom, dildo, chastity belt (here called 'Spanish padlock'), and tickler—on erotic toasts, on 'unnatural practices' (i.e. mouth-genital contacts), and on other lexicographical problems, as well as long lists of popular synonyms in the principal European languages for sex organs and sexual activities.

The word 'venery' has of course more than one meaning, and there is a tradition, probably apocryphal, that when this book first arrived at the BM, a gift from the compiler, it was classified with books on hunting.

III

A SHORT HISTORY OF THE PRIVATE CASE

FEW PEOPLE nowadays, passing into the British Museum reading room, look up at baron Carlo Marochetti's bust of Sir Anthony Panizzi which stands in a circular blue niche above the entrance, or read the brief account of Panizzi which accompanies the portrait of him on the corridor wall, almost opposite the lavatory for women readers. Yet this volatile and energetic man, who for thirty-five years worked sixteen hours a day in the service of the BM, transformed its library more than any other administrator before or since.

A lawyer by training, an Italian revolutionary democrat by temperament and conviction, Panizzi was sentenced to death in his absence by the despotic government of Modena, an Italian duchy then under Austrian domination. He settled in England in 1823, joined the BM staff in 1831, and became keeper of printed books in 1837, promoted through sheer ability over the head of his senior. For this and other reasons he was not greatly liked by some of his colleagues, at least one of whom dubbed him 'The Foreigner'. Others called him 'the Napoleon of librarians'.

Panizzi built up the library's holding of books from about 200,000 volumes in 1839 to about 1,250,000 on his retirement in 1866—partly through judicious purchases and partly through strict enforcement of the Copyright Act. It was he who, in 1845, secured an annual Treasury grant of £10,000 for the library, which he raised from sixth or seventh to first or second in the world. He could catalogue twice as many books a day as any of his colleagues, and the first general catalogue bears the stamp of his methods on every page. The magnificent domed reading room itself, occupying what had hitherto been an empty quadrangle and opened in 1857, was Panizzi's idea.

In 1835–36 a select committee of the House of Commons inquired into the condition, management, and affairs of the British Museum, and Panizzi, at that time 'extra assistant keeper', was one of the witnesses. He was asked whether the same facilities were given to the most obscure individual who visited the reading room as to the most celebrated and eminent readers. To illustrate his reply, he told the following story:

> Not long since a poor woman came to the Museum; she wanted a newspaper about an enclosure. Mr. Baber happened to be present when she was addressing herself to me, and he began to ask questions about the enclosure, what it was and where it was; he gave her not only the newspaper which she wanted, but a great deal of information how she was to go about it to get her rights properly guarded. If she had been a lord, the only thing would have been a bow on introducing him to the reading-room, and giving the newspaper, he would then have had to find out what he wanted by himself.

Allowing for some exaggeration in the final phrase, Panizzi's principles are summed up here as they are in his creed which I have put at the beginning of this book. He

37

wanted the great national library to be open to the poorest
student in the land. He wanted that student to have the
same means of indulging his curiosity on any topic, consulting all authorities, and 'fathoming the most intricate
inquiry', as the richest man in the kingdom. 'And I contend', he added, 'that Government is bound to give him
the most liberal and unlimited assistance in this respect.' So
far as he could, Panizzi put these principles into practice.
From him, indeed, stems one of the two opposing traditions, in the attitude towards readers and towards free
inquiry, which are apparent in the history of the BM
library over the past hundred years.

There have not only been two opposing traditions; there
have also been two very different types of administrator.
And in Panizzi's day the view that the BM library existed
to serve the learned and privileged few, while readers and
even museum visitors below a certain social level were
highly undesirable, was expressed most clearly by his pre-
decessor as principal librarian, Sir Henry Ellis (1777–
1869).

In all kinds of ways, Sir Henry was the polar opposite of
Sir Anthony. To start with, he was not gifted 'with any of
those salient abilities which dazzle the eyes of men', as
Edward Edwards puts it in his *Lives of the Founders of the
British Museum* (1870). He is said to have secured the post
of principal librarian, not on merit, but by running after
the carriage of the royal physician, Sir William Knighton,
whom he asked to put in a word for him with the king.
He is chiefly remembered as a cataloguer whose reputation
rather exceeded his achievements. When he gave evidence
before the 1835–36 select committee, Ellis bitterly opposed
any idea of opening the museum during public holidays,
declaring: 'I think that the most mischievous part of the

population is abroad and about at such a time.' The 'most vulgar class' would crowd into the museum and harm would be done. Indeed, if the museum were not closed altogether during the Easter and Whitsun holiday weeks, 'the place . . . would really be unwholesome'. He told the committee that soon after the reading room was first opened on Saturdays, a messenger came to him and said:

'Sir, there is great discontent in the reading room.'

'What has happened now?' asked Ellis.

'Why, sir,' replied the messenger, 'the fleas are inconveniencing the readers; the room wants washing.'

Ellis told the committee that 'people of a higher grade would hardly wish to come to the Museum at the same time with sailors from the dock-yards and girls whom they might bring with them. I do not think such people would gain any improvement from the sight of our collections.'

'Did you ever know', he was asked, 'an instance of a sailor bringing a girl from the dock-yards?'

'I never traced them to the dock-yards,' he admitted, 'but the class of people who would come at such times would be of a very low description.'

Asked about the possibility of opening the reading room in the evening, as had formerly been the practice, he said 'men of research' were content to read in the early part of the day, carry home the materials they had gathered, and write them up in the evening. He went on:

'I believe the Committee will find that a different class of readers would come to the Museum in the evening . . . they would be lawyers' clerks, and persons who would read voyages and travels, novels, and light literature; a class I conceive the Museum library was not intended for.'

'A merchant's or lawyer's clerk might have a literary taste?' he was asked. He replied:

'Yes; but the main purpose of a national library is to assist research: to aid those who are more professionally devoted to knowledge. Circulating libraries provide most of the books which merchants' clerks would want.'

Small wonder that Panizzi expressed himself stongly about Ellis. Unfortunately we have no record of what he said. Louis Fagan, his protégé and biographer, writes in the *Life of Sir Anthony Panizzi* (2nd edn, 1880): 'We prefer not to reproduce his remarks.'

Not that Ellis was alone in his views. Some other BM witnesses supported him. A certain John Flint South ventured to doubt whether the reading room would be used in the evening for more than novel-reading, while one R. Hannay complained that many of late had frequented the museum to read 'such books as *Tom Jones*, or Scott's novels; they are generally lads, and are a great annoyance to the studious'.

Now, the attitude customarily taken by BM officials towards the erotic material in their care, over the past hundred years, seems to reflect the Ellis rather than the Panizzi tradition. So I began to realize as I dug out the few historical references I could find to the BM collections of erotica. Gradually I began to piece together, so far as a non-member of the staff could, a history of the private case and of the protests it has engendered over the years. And I began to suspect that in the nineteenth century free inquiry into erotica at the BM was permitted to the rich, the privileged, the friends of trustees and officials, much more readily than to Panizzi's poor student. Nor did this state of affairs end with the nineteenth century.

I do not know the exact date when the private case was established. Neither, I am assured, does the principal keeper of printed books or anyone else in his department.

But I do not think it can have been before 1856. In that year Panizzi was promoted from keeper of printed books to principal librarian and John Winter Jones (1805–81) replaced him as keeper of printed books. I have never seen a book, now or formerly catalogued in the private case, bearing a BM accession stamp earlier than 1856; indeed, the earliest date I can remember seeing on such a book is 1857. This in itself is not proof, of course—though it is generally possible to see whether a book has had more than one pressmark and, if so, what the superseded one was. The earliest private case books all have the words 'Private Case' written out in full at the beginning of the pressmark; in all of them this early pressmark is erased and replaced by one beginning 'P.C.' Rarely is there an earlier pressmark still; with very few exceptions, it does not seem to have been the practice, in the early days, to transfer to the private case books already in the general catalogue. The private case was almost entirely for accessions. This led, incidentally, to the anomaly that not a few books, periodicals, and newspapers were admitted to the general catalogue in Panizzi's day, and remain there, which are far more obscene than many works which, some time after his promotion, were classified in the private case and omitted from the general catalogue.

These facts suggest that the omission of newly acquired erotic books from the general catalogue was a decision taken by John Winter Jones off his own bat about the year 1857. No exceptional flood of pornographic literature is recorded from the eighteen-fifties or -sixties. The Holywell Street boom had begun in the eighteen-thirties, and such publishers as William Dugdale (alias Henry Smith, alias James Turner, alias Charles Brown, alias Henry Young), who operated from several addresses in and near that street,

41

failed to send their productions to the BM under the Copyright Act, those of them which it possesses being acquired later. There was thus no compelling external reason for the authorities suddenly to start segregating erotic books and censoring the catalogue. Was Winter Jones the type of man to invent a private case to house books which shocked him or might shock critics of the BM administrators, if those critics came across their titles in the general catalogue? He was noted for his 'sound judgment' and 'dry reserve', and his chief contribution to knowledge, executed at the age of seventeen, was *A Translation of all the Greek, Latin, Italian, and French Quotations ... in Blackstone's Commentaries* (1823). He had been travelling secretary to the charity commissioners in the year *Oliver Twist* began publication. For years he had been Panizzi's right-hand man, and Panizzi was to remain his superior until 1866—though as principal librarian (an office renamed 'director and principal librarian' in 1898) 'The Foreigner' would be far less concerned with the day-to-day running of the department of printed books. Did Winter Jones, as keeper, decide to implement a long-cherished reform? Or did something make him take a sudden decision? Whichever it was, did he keep it secret from Panizzi?

I have been through the minutes of the BM trustees' standing committee and of the sub-committee on the library or, as it was renamed in the early eighteen-fifties, on printed books and manuscripts. In this early period, I can discover no reference to the private case. Yet all kinds of comparatively trivial things were reported to the trustees for their approval or decision, including the tiniest details of reading-room administration and of the mutilation and protection of books. Panizzi seems to have omitted nothing from his reports. The inference is that neither the trustees nor their principal librarian were told that certain books had been withheld from the general catalogue and that a private case had been inaugurated.

It would be less than candid to conceal that the late principal keeper thought little of this hypothesis when I put it to him. Winter Jones, he said, was very much Panizzi's creature and would have done nothing without his knowledge. Nevertheless Panizzi, though extremely influential, was not an absolute dictator; there were always officials who did not see eye to eye with him on various questions; and it is not inconsistent with the state of affairs at the museum in that period for Winter Jones to have taken an independent and secret decision concerning what was then, after all, a mere handful of books. For it was not, as we have seen, a question of reclassifying and removing from the catalogue whole shelves full, but of dealing discreetly with a few accessions.

My conjecture is, I think, supported by a small incident I discovered in the trustees' minutes for 1862–63. In 1862 a lawyer called Sir Thomas Phillips, a BM trustee who had made a name for himself shooting down chartists at Newport twenty years before, wrote to the Treasury objecting to the BM's having purchased sixty-eight chapbooks (popular pamphlets hawked by chapmen), printed in the sixteenth and seventeenth centuries, from J. O. Halliwell for the sum of £450. Phillips demanded a list of the books, and the standing committee told him he could call at the museum and see the bill, on which the titles were written. Whether he persevered with his objections after seeing them, I have been unable to discover; but I do know that the character of one at least of these chapbooks—or rather of Halliwell's 1861 reprint of it, in an edition of forty copies—had attracted the attention of a genial connoisseur of smut named Sir

William Hardman. What Phillips may have found disgusting, as well as disgustingly expensive, Hardman found 'boshy', but worth quoting. Though neither the original chapbook, beautifully bound, nor Halliwell's reprint of it went into the private case, it is possible that some such protest as Phillips's had put Winter Jones on his guard against allowing too much to leak out about the nature of certain accessions, of which he himself may not have altogether approved. In 1863, the museum acquired a copy of César Famin's profusely illustrated account of the erotic paintings, bronzes, and statues in the Royal Museum at Naples—the famous 'secret cabinet'—and this book did go into the private case. It is full of detailed pictures of various coital postures and of all kinds of non-coital sexual activity; one can imagine Winter Jones's reluctance to let Sir Thomas Phillips start bombarding the Treasury with letters about *that*.

To return for a moment to Sir William Hardman. His reference to one of the Halliwell chapbooks, in a letter written in March 1862, indicates a practice of not only permitting certain favoured readers to see 'curious' items, but of actually drawing their attention to accessions of this kind. Hardman (1828–90) gets no mention in the *Dictionary of National Biography*, but he was not a nobody. He was lawyer, magistrate, recorder, and friend of Meredith, and the three volumes (1923–30) of extracts from his letters and diaries contain some of the most fascinating and revealing documents of their kind and period.

At the British Museum the other day [he wrote to a friend] one of the attendants called my attention to a curious book—for my Pantagruelian fancies are well known to one or two of the Museum people—called

44

The Sack-full of Newes. It is a reprint of a very scarce and unique tract of 1673. Mr. J. O. Halliwell, F.R.S., has had 40 copies struck off. . . . *The Sack-full of Newes* consists of short stories and merry jests such as used to arride [*sc.* gratify] our ancestors. I need not say that most of them are terribly dry, and most boshy. There are two, however, which I will set down for your consolation, damn you!

There is a prim editorial footnote: 'The stories are omitted here.' In truth, they are hardly worth quoting; typical is the one about the man who dreamed that he was dead and in heaven, and 'that he did shite through the moon into the world, but he did shite into his wives lap'.

Four years after his reference to *The Sack-full of Newes*, Hardman was commenting on a proposal by 'some gentleman of the name of Witt' to present to the BM his collection of manuscripts, drawings, etc., illustrating the worship of Priapus:

> This collection is, I believe, the finest extant. His conditions are that a separate room be set apart for their reception, and that the public have access to them under certain restrictions. I don't know whether I should have the courage to apply for an order of admission, but I should very much like to look through the records of that noble 'cultus' quietly, if I could manage to do so by the intervention of my Museum friends.

Another privileged visitor, who must have had a few 'museum friends' too, wrote in 1875 that the objects left to the nation by George Witt and, before him, by the numismatist Richard Payne Knight (1750–1824), author of *A*

45

Discourse on the Worship of Priapus (1786), now formed one collection 'which, to the shame of the British Museum authorities, is consigned to a dark room in the basement, difficult of access, and where the interesting specimens it comprises can be inspected only under the greatest disadvantages'.

This complaint came from the pen of Henry Spencer Ashbee (1834–1900), rich business man—he left property valued at £63,000—traveller, book-collector, and bibliographer. Under the pseudonym 'Pisanus Fraxi' (a rearrangement of the letters in the Latin words for 'ash', *fraxinus*, and 'bee', *apis*) he compiled three monumental volumes of erotic bibliography, with copious extracts from the works described. These volumes were published privately in 1877, 1879, and 1885 under the common subtitle *Notes Bio- Biblio- Icono- graphical and Critical on Curious and Uncommon Books*. They are models of erudition and accuracy in a field noted for neither.

Ashbee says nothing of his relationship with the authorities in charge of the private case, and indeed makes certain criticisms of the museum, like the one just quoted. However, in 1875 he records that a copy of the original edition of Knight's 'masterly' *Discourse*, containing an extra plate showing a group of three male and two female figures engaged in fellatio, anal coitus, and intermammary contact (what Rowlandson called 'larking') is in the 'reserved library' of the British Museum. He also mentions private case copies of an anti-religious work in the form of dialogues between priests and whores, *Le Courrier extraordinaire des fouteurs ecclésiastiques* (Paris, 1790; reprinted 1872 and 1875); and of *Rare Verities: the cabinet of Venus unlocked, and her secrets laid open* (1658), a translation of part of *Geneanthropeiae: siue de hominis genera-*

46

tione (Rome, 1642) by the Italian primitive sexologist Giovanni Benedetto Sinibaldi (1594–1658), with such quaint chapter headings as 'Whether females may change their Sex', 'Which is most lustfull, a man or a beast', 'Which of the two is most lustfull, a Man or a Woman', 'How to inlarge the pudenda to a fit proportion', and 'Concerning some men that have had wonderful great Genitals'. Today's private case has a different copy of *Le Courrier extraordinaire* from the one Ashbee describes, but *Rare Verities* is still at the pressmark he quotes. There are several copies of its Latin original in the general library, and it and *The Crafty Whore* (1658), an imitation of the *Ragionamenti* (1534–36) of Pietro Aretino (1492–1556), are the earliest books printed in English to be found in the private case. In 1885, though with a slight error in the pressmark, Ashbee notes a private case copy—again, still to be found there—of a semi-erotic magazine, *The Rambler* (1824–25), one of many periodicals with similar titles and contents; this copy, he writes, is 'the only one which has passed through my hands'.

Enough has been said to show that Ashbee had access, if not to the private case catalogue, then at any rate to such works as he guessed were in the relatively small private case of those days and troubled to ask for. I am however inclined to suspect that the BM authorities understandably treated him with special consideration, as the owner of one of the world's finest collections of editions and translations of *Don Quixote*. It does not do to offend a collector of desirable books, if you are a librarian; he might change his will. In the event, Ashbee left his Cervantes collection to the BM together with his collection of erotic and semi-erotic books. This double-edged bequest was accepted and 15,229 volumes were transferred from Ashbee's house in

47

the Kent village of Hawkhurst, not far from Tunbridge Wells, and from his chambers in Gray's Inn. It is often said that the BM hesitated before accepting the Ashbee erotica; but there is no evidence of this in the minutes of the trustees' standing committee—though they did decide to destroy certain duplicates, a course sanctioned by Ashbee's will. Those erotica not destroyed were to be 'kept specially locked up'. It appears that a large number of duplicates, 'in a portion of the Ashbee collection . . . which had hitherto escaped examination', were not destroyed until 1914; about a hundred of these remaining duplicates were then considered to be 'of some value' and were therefore not destroyed but presented to the Bodleian library.

One cannot help wondering how many of the destroyed duplicates were copies of the astonishing number of works which have since, despite all the precautions, been 'mislaid'—i.e. stolen, by readers or staff—and which are in many cases irreplaceable.

Much has been made by writers on these topics of the fundamental importance of the Ashbee bequest for the private case. My own impression is that the Ashbee collection was much stronger in eighteenth-century semi-erotic or gallant literature than in what are properly described as erotic works of any period—and the gallant literature for the most part went into the general library, not the private case. However that may be, the three volumes of Ashbee's *Notes* describe, not only his own personal collection, but also books which had passed through his hands or through those of his collector and pornographer friend James Campbell Reddie (d. 1878), whose invaluable three-volume 'Bibliographical Notes on Books', another part of the Ashbee bequest, is in the BM's department of manuscripts (Add. MSS. 38828–30). Many an earnest inquirer has at first assumed that all the books described in Ashbee's bibliographies would be found in the private case. Not only are most of them not there: many of them, like most of the erotic literature of all ages and countries, have disappeared for ever. The Ashbee collection, then, cannot properly be called the 'nucleus' of the private case, though it was certainly a substantial addition to it.

One further gleam of light is thrown on the nineteenth-century private case, ten years before Ashbee's death, by an entry in the BM trustees' minutes for November 8, 1890. On that date the principal librarian laid before the board a letter written by a certain Mr W. J. Wilberforce to the archbishop of Canterbury, who had forwarded it for the trustees' consideration. The letter called attention to the annual expenditure of public money in the purchase for the museum of 'immoral books', chiefly printed abroad, and suggested 'that such books already bought should be destroyed and similar purchases discontinued for the future'. Mr Wilberforce, it turned out, had formerly been an assistant in the department of printed books 'and had officially to deal from time to time with the Catalogue of Private Case Books which were specially reserved from public use'. A report was also submitted from the recently appointed keeper of printed books, Richard Garnett (1835–1906), 'explaining the precautions observed by his predecessors and himself in dealing with printed works of the character specified by Mr. Wilberforce, both as to their limited acquisition on literary or other special grounds, and as to the restrictions imposed on their use, which is only permitted on direct proof of a legitimate purpose'. It was resolved that a copy of Garnett's report be sent to the archbishop, 'but not for communication to Mr. Wilberforce'. And the trustees declared themselves satisfied that all due precautions were exercised 'both in the acquisition of the literature to which Mr. Wilberforce calls attention and in the use which is allowed to be made of it'. So far as I am aware, this was the first time the trustees had ever discussed the question.

At this point, as we pass from the nineteenth century to the twentieth, I should like to summarize the argument of the present chapter so far. It is that the private case of the British Museum, consisting of books weighed in the balance and found wanton, was inaugurated and added to in a tradition of keeping such books as the preserve of a small circle of privileged men of letters, rich amateurs, and dilettanti. A rich collector like Ashbee did not depend on the goodwill of the British Museum, for he could afford to buy most of the books he wanted to read. Nor did the eroto-bibliomaniac Frederick Hankey (c. 1832–82) depend on the BM; this former Guards captain once told Ashbee how he had recovered from a serious illness by suddenly obtaining an edition of Sade's *Justine* which he had long sought in vain. Still less did Richard Monckton Milnes, Lord Houghton (1809–85) depend on the BM; he shared with Hankey, if the Goncourts are to be believed, a taste for torturing very young girls with pins and for witnessing hangings in the company of prostitutes ('He had many fine tastes and some coarse ones', says the *Dictionary of National Biography*) and was another indefatigable book collector, who enriched his library at Fryston Hall in Yorkshire with pornographic works procured for him by Hankey in Paris and smuggled across the Channel in the British diplomatic bag. In any case, Milnes himself became a trustee of the BM in 1881, having had to wait until the death of Panizzi, with whom he had quarrelled, before feeling free to accept the appointment. As trustee, he could browse to his heart's content in whatever erotic tit-bits the private case possessed which did not happen to be on his own shelves at Fryston Hall.

Above all, the small circle of collectors and amateurs were men who shared the same background and education as the higher officials of the BM. They had been to the same schools and universities; they were no doubt members of the same clubs, where erotica were freely accessible in the libraries, though perhaps chained to the shelves to prevent members' taking them home for closer study.* They shared the same aristocratic, civilized unshockability: the attitude so well expressed in John Buchan's description, in *Memory Hold-the-Door* (1940), of how Henry James and he examined the Byron archives of Lady Lovelace. 'During a summer week-end', wrote Buchan, 'Henry James and I waded through masses of ancient indecency, and . . . my colleague never turned a hair. His only words for some special vileness were "singular"—"most curious"—"nauseating, perhaps, but how quite inexpressibly significant".'

I should be the first to admit that this attitude towards certain areas of human behaviour has much in common with the scientific attitude. The difference, it seems to me, is this: the aristocratic—or Sir Henry Ellis—attitude is to restrict the masses of ancient indecency to gentlemen, to those who can be trusted not to turn a hair; the scientific— or Havelock Ellis—attitude is to put no barriers in the way of free inquiry.

The next we hear of the private case, in fact, after the

* A practice described in the *British Medical Journal* for March 30, 1963, where it is said to be still current. Henry Tedder (1850–1924), the Athenæum's librarian from 1874 to 1922, told E. S. P. Haynes of a club tradition that all male servants had to read a certain State trial; the appropriate volume was always having to be rebound.

special key turns on the Ashbee collection, is in connexion with the writings of Havelock Ellis (1859–1939) and his fellow sexologist Edward Carpenter (1844–1929). The treatment the pair of them sustained at the hands of the BM just before the first world war caused them to protest in the pages of the *English Review*. Their article was called 'The Taboos of the British Museum Library', and it was written in collaboration with the lawyer E. S. P. Haynes (1877–1949). His signature alone appeared on it because its main purpose was to protest against the exclusion of books by Ellis and Carpenter from the general catalogue.

This article, which was published in December 1913, is the most important single document throwing light on the history of the private case, for it shows how BM practice in that year affected men of science; and the picture it painted was to hold good in essentials for another fifty years.

Three general classes of book, said the Haynes article, were liable to be buried by the BM: books (1) subversive of the throne, (2) subversive of religion, and (3) of an improper or obscene character. Ellis's *Studies in the Psychology of Sex* (1905, etc.), a monumental work in six volumes on all phases of the sexual question, had been offered to the keeper of printed books on condition that it should be rendered accessible; the reply was that the six volumes would be accepted, but would not be placed in the catalogue. So they were not sent. A keeper of printed books might not be able to reconcile his conscience to the thought of placing a wicked and naughty book in a reader's hands; but to refuse to let the reader know of the existence of such a book (lest it be obtained elsewhere) argued a superhuman anxiety for his eternal welfare. The originals of some foreign works were admitted to the catalogue, though the English translations were barred. Why should a great library take sides in religious controversy and bury G. W. Foote's *Illustrated Bible*? Miscellaneous volumes vaguely classified as 'rubbish' were also suppressed, as were 'free-spoken works of historical interest about the Royal Family' and Edward Carpenter's *Intermediate Sex* (1908). The latter had been favourably reviewed in various educational and medical journals, but when Carpenter wrote to the newly appointed keeper of printed books, Arthur W. Kaye Miller (1849–1914), asking why it had not appeared in the catalogue five years after publication, he received the reply: 'Dear Sir,—As the above book is only available upon special application it has not been entered in the catalogue.' Carpenter asked why; and what were the conditions and method of special application; and the following letters were exchanged:

The keeper to Carpenter:

Dear Sir,—In your letter of the 12th July, referring to books which are not entered in the catalogue, you ask me whether there are any printed instructions issued, and available for public use, by which the public may know of the existence of such books, and of the conditions under which they may be consulted. My reply to your question is that there are no printed instructions relating to such books.

Carpenter to the keeper:

Dear Sir,—I am obliged for your letter of the 15th inst. I gather from it and the former correspondence that my book and a large number of other serious works on various subjects are not entered in the general catalogue, but are to be had 'upon special applica-

53

tion'. May I now ask what the procedure of 'special application' is, and how the public may obtain information as to what books can be consulted in that way?

The keeper to Carpenter:

Dear Sir,—I have to acknowledge the receipt of your letter of the 23rd July. The question which you ask has, I think, been sufficiently answered in my former letters, to which I have no further information to add.

I am told that the curtness of this final letter may perhaps be explained by the fact that in 1913—and until surprisingly recently—it was not thought necessary for the correspondence of the keeper of printed books to be done on one of those new-fangled typewriters. His letters were written, and copied by hand. Miller retired in the following February and died suddenly soon afterwards.

A further substantial addition to the private case, less celebrated than the Ashbee bequest, was made in February 1920. The chancellor of the duchy of Lancaster, the 27th earl of Crawford (1871–1940), presented 200 erotic books to the BM, 'for preservation or destruction at the discretion of the Trustees', and two months later it was decided to destroy certain duplicates and retain the rest. The earl was himself a trustee of the British Museum.

About twenty years after the publication of 'The Taboos of the British Museum Library', Haynes told the British Society for the Study of Sex Psychology that the situation had not greatly changed since 1913. He recalled being in the BM reading room and hearing an eminent author (unnamed) demand to see 'the bawdy books'. This author

54

was tired of reading about Wordsworth and wanted something more piquant.

> Of course [said Haynes] the officials denied their existence, though everyone knows they are there; but I really cannot see why an honest man of letters who wants to see bawdy books (which are, after all, national property, although they have been illegally destroyed from time to time) should not see them, or why any tax-payers who are admitted to the British Museum reading room should not be allowed to see them.

Mr Alec Craig, in *The Banned Books of England* (1937), recorded an interview with 'a blushing young gentleman' at the British Museum, who had to satisfy himself that Mr Craig was a fit and proper person to see Charles Knowlton's birth control manual *Fruits of Philosophy* (1832). Mr Craig listed obscenity, blasphemy, betrayal of masonic secrets, and unseemly truthfulness about royal families as reasons for the removal of books from the public catalogue. He returned to the subject in *Above All Liberties* (1942). Only the most persistent inquiries, he wrote, would establish the existence of copies of John Roberton's *Generative System* (4th edn, 1817; 5th edn, 1824) in the BM library (the 1811 edition, which does not have the plates, is in the general catalogue). The practice of excluding certain books from the catalogue was a serious matter.

> Many of the books so excluded are of important literary, historical and scientific interest. The guileless reader who relies on the catalogue is left in complete ignorance of their existence; and, what is more, the

55

value of the published catalogue as a bibliographical work is greatly impaired to the detriment of subscribers all over the world.

Norman E. Himes, in the introduction to his great *Medical History of Contraception* (1936), complained that to secure access to the BM's 'special cabinet for certain books' required not only serious purpose but tact, patience, and persistence. 'Some amusing stories', he wrote, 'could be related of these experiences.' Unfortunately, he did not relate them.

And there, except for similar references by Mr Craig in *The Times Literary Supplement* for March 1, 1957, and in his *Banned Books of England and Other Countries* (1962), matters rested until the spring of 1963, when the principal keeper of printed books was at last stung into a public justification of the private case. Less than two years later, however, it was decided to incorporate titles of private case books in the general catalogue. But before discussing the trustees' partial 'modernization', as they are pleased to call it, let us see what the fuss is about. Just what has been locked up in the private case for all these years?

IV

SEXOLOGY, DICTIONARIES, AND
BOOKS ABOUT BOOKS

IN THIS and the next four chapters I shall give some account of the contents of the private case. I shall show what kind of literature has evoked, for a hundred years, such powerful taboos in its custodians. I shall do so as dispassionately as possible when writing about questions few of us, even if we are not librarians, can remain altogether detached from. This conducted tour through the dirty book department will have to be highly selective. I should have liked to mention a great many more books, but it seemed to me that few readers would find much of interest in a mere list of titles, quaint though some of them are. Experts may deplore the lack of bibliographical detail and the undue attention to English works at the expense of the usually better-written foreign ones. But I am writing for lay readers, who no doubt want some idea of what these books are about rather than what they look like, and who all read English. And I am compiling, for separate publication, a catalogue of the English books in the private case, into which the experts will be able to get their teeth; and then, it is to be hoped, someone will undertake a similar catalogue of the foreign-language works.

There are, broadly speaking, three kinds of sexology:

primitive, or pre-scientific; more or less scientific; and popular. All three kinds are represented in the private case.

A good example of primitive or folk sexology surviving in near-chapbook form well into the nineteenth century is William Dugdale's 1832 edition of *The Secrets of Nature Revealed*, a translation of part of *Physionomia* by the thirteenth-century Scottish savant Sir Michael Scot or Scott. It should be compared, on the one hand, with the work of Sinibaldi referred to in the previous chapter; on the other, with the various editions of pseudo-Aristotle, called *Aristotle's Master Piece*, etc. *The Secrets of Nature Revealed* sums up medieval notions of sexual hygiene and reproduction. Excessive venery caused 'frequent meagrims', but moderate venery was good for all of a sanguine complexion. Women of a hot constitution had small breasts; much hair about the privities, occasioned by the extraordinary heat in those parts; short, curly hair on their heads; shrill, loud voices; and irregular menstrual periods. A child's sex depended on which testicle the seed had come from: 'from the right testicle cometh the male, and from the left the female'. Women readers were told the signs of conception and given remedies against barrenness: yellow rape-seed (*Brassica campestris oleifera*) baked in bread, for instance. Not the least interesting thing about Dugdale's edition is the demand for sex education its publication reveals. Its wretched printing, paper, and wrapper, its irrelevant gaudy frontispiece, are typical of Dugdale's shoddy productions, which one historian of erotica, who has clearly never seen any of them, describes as splendid, exquisite, and handsome.

J. D. T. de Bienville's *Nymphomania, or, a dissertation concerning the furor uterinus* (1775), a translation by Edward Sloane Wilmot of *La Nymphomanie* (Amsterdam, 1771), is primitive sexology masquerading as science. The author, an M.D., recounts, with every appearance of sincerity, how he treated the 21-year-old Leonora by swathing her in bandages at night so that she could not touch her genitals; throwing cold water in her face when she uttered obscenities; blooding her; fitting a lead plate over her loins; injecting an infusion of herbs into her vagina; and putting syrup of poppies into her food. This is a less celebrated anti-masturbation tract than its inspirer, *L'Onanisme* (Lausanne, 1760) by Simon André de Tissot, an English version of which—*A Treatise on the Crime of Onan* (1766) —stands on the same private case shelf as Bienville's book. Tissot had great influence, and did much harm, throughout the nineteenth century. His book may justly be called seminal.

The outstanding work of early scientific sexology in English to be found in the private case is a beautifully bound copy of *Kalogynomia, or the laws of female beauty* (1821) by T. Bell, M.D., with twenty-four detailed anatomical plates. Bell, who gives a lucid description of the sex organs and their functioning, knew what the manufacturers of axillary and vaginal deodorants would have us forget: that 'the musky odour ... of the arm-pits and generative parts (and they are perfectly musky in cleanly persons of warm temperament) is a powerful stimulus to sexual love'. He is a thorough-going philosophical materialist, who finds it ridiculous to assert that there is any more crime in two persons of opposite sex mixing two drops of albumen in the sexual embrace than there would be in their mixing two drops of saliva by spitting on the same piece of ground. He boldly attacks his countrymen's double standard of morality: 'Even in England, we find an infinite number of men, who, vaunting the chastity of their own wives, have the vanity to hint at their irresistibility and their success with all other women.'

Julius Rosenbaum's *Plague of Lust, being a history of venereal disease in classical antiquity* (Paris, 1901), translated from the German by Alfred Allinson, is a work of exceptional erudition, which may still be read with profit. It was issued, in an edition of 500 copies, by the erotica publisher Charles Carrington, whose real name may have been Paul Ferdinando, and about whom some curious information is gathered in Mr Gershon Legman's *The Horn Book* (New Hyde Park, N.Y., 1964). Rosenbaum had an exhaustive knowledge of obscure Greek and Roman authors and gives a vivid picture of phallic worship, brothels, homosexuality, and other aspects of sexual behaviour in classical times. There is a useful bibliography. *The Manual of Classical Erotology* (1887 and 'Manchester, 1884' [i.e. Paris? 1899]), in two different translations from the *Apophoreta*, written in Latin, of Friedrich Carl Forberg (1770–1848), is a similar but more outspoken work, offering one of the earliest attempts at a scientific classification of sexual activity. Ninety 'erotic postures' are enumerated, from '1. The man face downwards taking between his thighs the woman, who lies on her back with her legs stretched out straight' up to '90. Group of five copulators.' One wonders why he stops at five. The BM received, as part of the Dawes bequest, a superb edition of Forberg (Paris, '1907' [*c.* 1922?]) with twenty charming plates. But for crazy multiplication of coital postures, there is nothing to beat the second volume of 'Dr L. van der Weck-Erlen' (i.e. Josef Weckerle), *Das goldene Buch der Liebe* (Vienna, 1907), where, in 303 pages, no fewer than 531 different positions are described, classified, and given names.

These works are of no little importance in the history of sexology, a subject yet to receive its Macaulay. Coming to modern sexologists, we may mention another translation from the German: E. Heinrich Kisch's *Sexual Life of Woman* [1910], a solid work written exclusively from the masculine point of view. As was usual at the time, it plays down female homosexuality, which Kisch believes to be found chiefly 'among the ladies of the aristocracy'. A contemporary pamphlet going some way towards balancing this defect—here I am anticipating chapter VIII—is by an American medical man: Douglas C. McMurtie's *Some Observations on the Psychology of Sexual Inversion in Women*, offprinted from *The Lancet-Clinic* of November 2, 1912. It is a brief pioneering sketch of a subject for which there had hitherto been a shortage of illustrative material; its ten case histories include that of a lesbian prostitute whose two lovers were male homosexuals, 'chorus men in a musical show'. It is surprising to find in the private case another pioneering American work: Gilbert Van Tassel Hamilton's *A Research in Marriage* (New York, 1929), a brilliant anticipation of Kinsey and Masters, with an analysis of the sexual histories of a hundred married men and a hundred married women in New York city. Some pages of this copy were still uncut early in 1966, which shows how effectively it has been buried; but there is a copy of a later edition (1948) in the general library.

No account of the private case holding of scientific works would be complete without a mention of Edward Charles's famous *Introduction to the Study of the Psychology and Physiology and Bio-Chemistry of the Sexual Impulse among Adults in Mental and Bodily Health* (1935). It is an irritating book. It includes much that is highfalutin and much that is highly technical. But there is also a plainly written and helpful, if somewhat poetical, exposition of coital technique and of the correlation of contraceptive technique with coital posture. Charles's book was prosecuted and sup-

61

pressed as obscene, in spite of the evidence of sixteen expert witnesses, among them Julian Huxley, Janet Chance, Cecil I. B. Voge, Bronislaw Malinowski, J. B. S. Haldane, and Robert Briffault. Its suppression seems to have been largely due to its advocacy of open-air as against bedroom coition, and of coition during menstruation. It is high time it was reprinted.

The first popular sexologist of any note was a French writer of travel books and adventure novels called Louis Jacolliot (1837–90). Born in Charolles, he travelled widely and lived for many years in Chandernagore and Tahiti. His writings on sex, published under the pseudonym 'Dr Jacobus X . . .', are one of the three seemingly inexhaustible quarries—the others being Ashbee and Bloch—which later compilers of sex encyclopaedias and the like have freely, and pretty uncritically, pillaged. To be sure, Jacolliot is a mere compiler, like his imitators and plagiarists, believing everything he is told, adding only wild generalizations and wilder prejudices. But he at least indicates his sources. With the BM's recent purchase of *The Basis of Passional Psychology* (Paris, 1901) on my suggestion, when a copy turned up for £4 in a London bookseller's catalogue, the private case now has all his sexological writings that have been translated into English. They were issued by Carrington in Paris at the turn of the century, in quick succession.

The private case has two editions of Jacolliot's *The Ethnology of the Sixth Sense: studies and researches into its abuses, perversions, follies, anomalies, and crimes*, one published in 1899, the other in the following year. This work concerns the anatomy of the genital organs of both sexes— their structure, singularities, diseases, defects, malformations, mutilations, and amputations—and contains some remarkable stories and case histories. The still current joke is quoted in which a sergeant with one testicle bets a recruit that they have an odd number between them, but loses: the recruit has a supernumerary testicle, 'and with yours, that makes four'. Another chestnut in this book tells of the man who fell into the sea nine miles from shore. He floated on his back, thought of his sweetheart, and fashioned a sail out of his handkerchief. Here too is the celebrated anecdote of 'the split penis of the shepherd Galien and his masturbating stick', which one encounters in far more recent and respectable manuals. Section headings include: 'Mutilation of the penis by the teeth of a convict, followed by the murder of the victim'; 'Profound despondency of the unfortunate persons who have lost their penis'; 'Penis found in the stomach of a dog'; and 'Monstrous clitores'. There is an agreeable sprinkling of tourists' tales: a woman who inserts a bottle in her vagina, from which visitors may drink if so disposed; a cook who inserts hard-boiled eggs into his rectum for a purpose which I cannot, I fear, recall.

This book has two supplements: *The Genital Laws* (1901), in which there is special emphasis on coital postures and on impotence; and *Medico-Legal Examination of the Abuses, Aberrations and Dementia of the Genital Sense* (1900), a kind of popular rewriting of Krafft-Ebing, dealing with such rare fancies as the glass stool used in Paris brothels —of the first class, be it understood—on which the whore defecated while the client lay underneath, observing at close but comfortable quarters the movements of the sphincter.

Perhaps Jacolliot's most interesting work is *L'Amour aux colonies* (1893), which is in the private case together with the second edition (1898) of a two-volume English translation: *Untrodden Fields of Anthropology: observations on the esoteric manners and customs of semi-civilized*

63

peoples, illustrated with meretricious plates of naked women. The author discusses Asian, African, and Polynesian sexual behaviour in copious and sometimes uproarious detail. Prostitution in the Chinese 'flower-boats' is described, but the European reader is warned never to expect any 'refinement of voluptuousness' from a Chinese girl: 'she only knows how to lie down and take you passively'. Under the heading 'Vicious habits of old Chinese debauchees', Jacolliot describes how, 'when the senses of an old Chinaman are so worn out that all natural means of excitement cannot arouse his enervated genital organs', he will witness an act of copulation between a 'strong coolie' and a woman, after which he 'eagerly receives *in bucca sua*, the liquid which runs *e vulva fœminæ*'. A brief bibliography of this 'strange freak of eroticism' is obligingly provided. Oriental aphrodisiacs and 'lewd contrivances' are listed, including the Chinese 'masturbating ball' and 'anal violin'.

Turning to the Negro race, Jacolliot, incapable of resisting a pat generalization, finds that while the Negro woman is usually of a passionate nature, she does not care to waste time in trifles, least of all such trifles as lesbianism and sodomy. In Guiana, she brings her lover to concert pitch by making him drink a preparation of 'tightening wood' (nux vomica bark) or clapping on his penis a 'hot aubergine'. This is a kind of irritating plaster, including pepper, applied eight or ten hours before copulation and producing 'an almost permanent erection at the least touch'. Erotic dances in Senegal and Tahiti are described, and the author interviews his 30-year-old washerwoman, a coloured lady of generous disposition, who claimed to have satisfied a sergeant and fifteen sharpshooters in a single night.

Untrodden Fields contains a great many irrelevancies, including a list of French slang expressions for different types of whore and excursus on opium, rape, necrophilia, lesbian orgies, and bestiality with a she-goat. With this work can profitably be compared George A. Turner's well-informed and temperate *Report on the Alleged Prevalence of Pulmonary Tuberculosis . . . in the Kraals of the Natives in Portuguese East African Territory* (Johannesburg, 1907), the second part of which is typewritten and illustrated with scores of photographs. A manuscript note at the front says the book was offered to the Guildhall library in 1910, but the committee 'declined the gift as it shocked their modesty'. The writer adds: 'Silly fools'. The subjects discussed and illustrated include dances miming coition, circumcision rites, female initiation rites, and hermaphrodism.

Another important group of serious or semi-serious works in the private case consists of dictionaries of sexual slang and colloquialisms. Erotic lexicography is a neglected subject in this country and those writers, including myself, who have ventured into it or touched its fringes have all been guilty of failing to trace many words and phrases to origins far more remote than we suspected possible. The French have always taken the subject more seriously, and a French friend of mine, a philologist, is carrying out research under the auspices of the Sorbonne into the past and present sexual slang of Englishmen. His work is expected to take ten years.

French sexual vocabulary was extensively studied, in the middle of the last century, in two works published in Brussels and a third in Paris. The *Glossaire érotique de la langue française* (1861) of 'Louis de Landes' (i.e. Jean Auguste Udalric Scheler) goes from *abailardiser* ('Mettre quelqu'un dans l'état où le chanoine Fulbert mit Abailard') to *voix* ('employé dans un sens obscène pour designer la vigueur vénérienne'). The BM copy contains manuscript notes by Ashbee. A similar and closely imitative work is the *Dictionnaire érotique moderne* 'par un professeur de langue verte' (i.e. Alfred Delvau), published by Jules Gay in 1864 with the false imprint: 'Freetown, Imprimerie de la Bibliomaniac Society'. Then there is *Le Petit Citateur* ('Paphos' [i.e. Paris], 1869) by 'J.-Ch-x, bachelier ès mauvaises langues'. All three are chock-full of illustrative quotations from French erotic writings. In 1896 that much borrowed-from student of English slang John Stephen Farmer published anonymously a conflation of these three dictionaries, with English equivalents supplied for the headwords, under the title *Vocabula amatoria*. It begins with *abandonner (s')* ('to surrender oneself to the sexual embrace: of women only') and ends with *zon (faire)* ('1. to copulate. Also (2) to sodomise'). Farmer's compilation is an untrustworthy guide, since he systematically ignores the finer shades of meaning in the French and chooses English slang equivalents quite arbitrarily.

Henry N. Cary's *Slang of Venery* (1916) was mentioned in chapter II. There is a kind of modest supplement to it, *Americana sexualis* (1939), compiled by 'Justinian'. This concentrates on American expressions, from *around-the-world* ('a form of sexual activity in which the female lies passive upon her back while the male stimulates her . . . with successive kisses, caresses, and massages upon the neck, shoulders, breasts, stomach', etc.) to *wolf* ('a man who adopts the dominant role in sodomy or *penis in ora*; a man who seduces young girls . . . Becoming a euphemism'). 'Justinian' suffers from that besetting sin of lexicographers, pomposity. Take, for instance, his definition of *daisy chain*: 'Virtually the moral and aesthetic nadir of indiscriminate and variegated sexual activity within a bisexual social group . . . a melange of normal and perverted sexual conduct in an extremely heteromorphous manner. . . .'

Finally, some of the encyclopaedias, histories of erotica, and bibliographies that repose in the private case. All serious research in the field of sexual studies begins, or ought to begin, with the magnificent four-volume *Bilder-Lexikon* (Vienna and Leipzig, 1928–31), edited by Leo Schidrowitz. The set at Cambridge university library was brought through the Customs in a parcel marked 'Bible Lexicon'. The first volume discusses cultural history; the second, erotic literature and art; the third, sexual science. The fourth, largely bibliographical, volume is wanting from the BM set and missing from the set at Cambridge. Giuseppe Lo Duca's *Dictionnaire de sexologie* (Paris, 1962) is a pale imitation, and none too accurate.

Unlike the Bodleian library, the BM unfortunately does not possess Paul Englisch's magisterial *Geschichte der erotischen Literatur* (Stuttgart and Berlin, 1927), though a copy of the same author's very rare *Irrgarten der Erotik* (Leipzig, 1931), destroyed by the Nazis, was purchased recently. There is in the private case an *'adaptation française'* by Jacques Gorvil of the former work, entitled *L'Histoire de l'érotisme en Europe* (Paris, 1933), but I am unable to recommend it. Much may be learnt however from Bernhard Stern's *Illustrierte Geschichte der erotischen Literatur aller Zeiten und Völker* (Vienna and Leipzig, 1908); though not so comprehensive as the title suggests, this is a solid pioneering survey, with chapters on eroticism in the Bible and the Talmud. For English works it can be supplemented by the sketchy but useful *Om erotisk og galant Litteratur* (Copenhagen, 1948) by 'Pierre Marteau', which has a piquantly illustrated section on erotic bookplates.

The seeker after this and other kinds of erotic picture will find in the private case the profusely illustrated volumes of Eduard Fuchs (1870–1947); the less famous but much franker *Die Erotik in der Kunst* (Vienna and Leipzig, 1908) by Cary von Karwath; and the wider-ranging and altogether admirable *Kærlighedens Billedbog* (Copenhagen, 1956–59) by Ove Brusendorff and Poul Henningsen, translated by H. B. Ward and Elsa Gress as *Love's Picture Book* (Copenhagen, 1959–62). In these works may be studied otherwise inaccessible representations of the act of sex by Rembrandt, Rubens, Goya, and many other artists.

Of the erotic bibliographies in the private case, I have already mentioned Ashbee's three much-quoted volumes and Rose's *Registrum*, restricted for the sole reason that it lists private case works and supplies their pressmarks. There is also Ashbee's interleaved copy, with his manuscript notes, of the *Bibliographie des ouvrages relatifs à l'amour, aux femmes, au mariage* (2nd edn, Paris, 1864), by 'M. le C. d'I***' (i.e. Jules Gay). The key to *L'Enfer de la Bibliothèque nationale* is the volume of that name compiled by 'Guillaume Apollinaire' (i.e. Wilhelm Kostrowitsky), Fernand Fleuret, and Louis Perceau, and published in Paris in 1913; the private case has also a type-written supplement of *Enfer* accessions up to 1934, the titles having been supplied to Rose by officials of the *Bibliothèque nationale*. Perceau's two-volume *Bibliographie du roman érotique au xixe siècle* (Paris, 1930), presented to the BM in 1934 by Rose 'as a very slight tribute of appreciation of much help and kindness' (*viz*, permitting him to copy the private case catalogue), is a model of bibliographical perfection that has reduced at least one later worker to near-despair of ever being able to emulate it. Superbly organized, for all normal purposes complete, and possessing no fewer than eight indexes (titles, authors, editions, statistics, reprints, library and private collectors' holdings, imprints, and names), this is an indispensable tool of research.

Perceau is alone among bibliographers of erotica in making full use of clandestine catalogues. The private case now has a rich collection of such catalogues and prospectuses, in English and French, dating from the turn of the century and including Carrington's important *Bibliotheca arcana* (1899), which describes about 170 publications. These catalogues and prospectuses are to be found in 'Album 7', an Army and Navy Stores photograph album in which are mounted some eighty items from the collection of the late George Mountbatten, 2nd marquess of Milford Haven (1892-1938). Among them are leaflets and booklets advertising artificial genitalia, aphrodisiacs, tickler condoms, and erotic photographs; such photographs, I am told, fill the first six albums in the series, the present whereabouts of which are not known to me.

Erotic bibliography is a subject bristling with difficulties. The books it is concerned with are published, for the most part, clandestinely and in tiny editions. Imprint and date are often false or omitted. The author's real name is almost never given. Many of the books survive only in one or two copies, privately owned—or do not survive at all. The laborious elucidation of such problems is not only fascinating in itself but also of some value to sexologists, anthropologists, historians, and psychologists. It cannot be said that the attitude of the British Museum authorities has ever been particularly helpful to those who occupy themselves with these matters. Only two bibliographers, so far as I know, have ever been given access to the private case catalogue. One of these died soon afterwards; the other has never published his bibliography.

V

THE SEVENTEENTH AND EIGHTEENTH CENTURIES

MOST PEOPLE'S first reaction, on examining a typical seventeenth- or eighteenth-century private case book, would be to exclaim: 'How dull!' And indeed few seekers after sensation would find much to excite them in these bucolic miscellanies, jesters, Atalantises, chronicles, annals, and 'natural histories' of this and that. Which is not to say they are without interest to historians, for instance, or philologists, or students of minor literature. But it is not only a crime against scholarship to have kept them out of the catalogue and subject indexes for anything from sixty to a hundred years. It is a bad joke.

One wonders whether anyone actually read these books before condemning them to the arch room inferno. And whether perennial lack of competent staff, or of interest, or of intelligence, or of all three, has prevented, as the decades went by, any reconsideration of their fate. Some pre-1800 private case books were rehoused by their keepers, about forty or fifty years ago. They were put in yet another of these cabbalistic classifications: Tab. 603 to 605. A member of the staff once told me that these reprieved books, for which a superintendent's signature is needed, are kept 'in a cage'. Perhaps their bites are not poisonous; private case books are kept behind glass. But on what principles did the keepers decide to rehouse some and not others? There seems no logic in their choice. And have there been no scholars, well versed in the literature of the seventeenth and eighteenth centuries, to grow angry at the injustice done to harmless books and tell the museum authorities roundly that they were making asses of themselves? 'A book is not a book, if it is not read.' Our national library imprisons books without trial, without a single expert witness from outside the museum being heard in their defence, and in some cases, it seems, on the strength of their titles alone.

What Jack in office, for instance, put *Whipping-Tom: or, a rod for a proud lady* (1722) in the private case? This is a pamphlet chiding women for taking snuff, drinking 'debilitating' tea, walking in red cloaks like soldiers, and immodestly wearing hoop-petticoats, 'the screen for great bellies'. Whoever found more indelicacy in this than in a hundred other pamphlets of that period—the works of Tom Brown (1663–1704), for instance—must have been an inveterate but ill-read smut-snuffler. I can only suppose the book was thought to be something to do with the 'Whipping Tom' who roamed the London streets towards the end of the seventeenth century, pulling up women's skirts and spanking their bottoms.

The 1885 reprint of *The Philosophy of Pleasure; or, the history of a young lady*, originally published in 1774, is another book that seems to be in the private case solely on account of its title-page, which promises 'many and various luscious scenes'—unless the heroine's name, Fanny Ramsay, had something to do with it. At all events, here is one of these 'luscious scenes':

Sir George so presumptuously abused the consent he

had forced from me, that Nature prevailing over honour and anger in my breast, I suffered his wanton play, and connived at his audacious attempts. Sir George knew how to conquer, but not how to make use of his victory. At the very minute I lay panting in his arms, favouring his triumph, rather than opposing it, he discreetly declined the completing my defeat, that he might, as he said, enjoy with an undisturbed delight, all the advantages of it. The respite he gave restored to me my reason—I approved his resolution—and he went away.

The door was immediately locked and bolted, and I stepped into my bed, cursing my sensibility, and bewailing the cruelty of my fate. It was not long before Sir George came: his surprise was as great as the hope he had fondly indulged. He begged, prayed, intreated; I was inflexible and silent. 'What a fool I have been!' exclaimed he with an oath. And he tiptoed to his room, damning me, himself, the day he had seen me, and the credulity that had deprived him of happiness.

This book could well have been transferred to the general library two or three years ago, when the not dissimilar *Memoirs of a Coxcomb* (1751) by John Cleland (author of *Fanny Hill*) was belatedly removed from the private case.

Again, what incorrigible bibliotaph buried *The Fruit-shop* (1765), a kind of history of women, a singularly un-erotic work which discusses, in the longest-winded manner imaginable, such topics as 'Why most married Women, in imitation of Venus, are fond of military Seducers', and which takes 119 pages, or a quarter of the whole book, to get Adam and Eve expelled from Eden? There is a duplicate copy in the general library; the secret must be that the private case copy contains a frontispiece, missing from the other, showing a phallomorphic yew tree which two Cupids are about to crown with a vulva-shaped garland. To any reader who happens to possess a sex organ of either shape, there is nothing in the slightest degree shocking or offensive or titillating about this piece of naïve symbolism; yet it was deemed unsuitable for the eyes of the comparative handful of students who would be interested enough to send for 'another copy' if they saw it entered in the general catalogue. This is a crime against bibliography, which is concerned with, amongst other things, the examination and description of variant copies.

The Fruit-shop is only one of a large number of private case books, from these two centuries, which consist, in title and text, of extended sexual metaphor. Most frequently the female sex organs are represented as a country, with its peculiar customs, vegetation, and produce. Thus Ἐρωτόπολις: *the present state of Betty-land* (1684), attributed to the Staffordshire poet Charles Cotton (1630–87), begins:

> The Country of *Betty-land* is a Continent adjoyning to the Isle of *Man*, having the Island of *Man* wholly under its Jurisdiction. . . . For Tillage the Soyl is so proper, . . . that . . . men take the greatest pleasure in the world to plow it and sow it, nay there are some men that take it for so great a pastime, that they will give some a thousand some two thousand pounds a year for a little spot in that Country, not so big as the palm of your hand.

A little of that, for most readers, goes a very long way; and Ἐρωτόπολις continues in much the same vein for 181 pages. This kind of thing can however be seen as a primitive form of sex education; and from that point of view it is not without interest. The description of 'Betty-land' was reprinted, in a shortened form, in *The Potent Ally: or succours from Merryland* (2nd edn, 'Paris' [i.e. London], 1741), by 'Philo-Britanniæ', one of a series of booklets mostly by Thomas Stretser, whom the erotica publisher Edmund Curll (1675–1747) hacked. Stretser wrote *A New Description of Merryland* (1740) by 'Roger Pheuquewell, Esq.' and *Merryland Displayed* (1741), as well as two parodies of Philip Miller's *Catalogus plantarum* (1730): *The Natural History of the Arbor vitæ, or, Tree of Life* (1732; reprinted, 1741), all about the penis; and *The Natural History of the Frutex vulvaria* (1732; reprinted, 1741, as by 'Philogynes Clitorides'), whose title sufficiently indicates its subject. Other works of the same kind in the private case are: *Little Merlin's Cave: as it was lately discover'd, by a gentleman's gardener, in Maidenhead-thicket* (4th edn, 1737); *Teague-Root Display'd* (1746) by 'Paddy Strong-Cock'; *Wisdom Revealed; or, the tree of life discover'd and describ'd* [*c.* 1750] by 'a Studious Enquirer into the Mysteries of Nature'; *The Electrical Eel* [*c.* 1770] and *Mimosa: or, the sensitive plant* (1779), attributed to James Perry; and *La Souricière: the mousetrap* (1794) by 'Timothy Touchit, Esq.' One quotation will be enough, I think, and I have chosen *Little Merlin's Cave* because it is not too long to quote in full. The reader will perhaps ask himself why, three years after the legal publication in London of Henry Miller's *Tropic of Cancer*, this mild and charming piece of bawdy is solemnly buried by the BM authorities as if it would set its readers' loins on fire:

As blue-ey'd KATE, sweet-blooming buxom Maid,
With Gard'ner HARRY sat in lonely Shade,

74

Have you, cry'd she, dear HARRY, ever seen,
The Cave of MERLIN, rais'd near *Richmond-Green*?
No, answer'd HAL; but in this very Wood,
There is a Cave that's every Whit as good:
'T has Shrubs and Bushes all without, within
'Tis Crimson Velvet, soft as th' Ermin's Skin.
A Spring it has, give Rapture to the Touch,
That never flows too little or too much:
All that old Poets feigns of Scenes of Bliss,
In ev'ry single Point comes short of this.

Where is it, HARRY, where? cries eager KATE,
I long to prove the Wonders you relate.
The Door, said HAL, 's the Place whereon you sit,
Fall back, and on the very Spot I'll hit:
But with this Rod a Circle first describe,
Shall make th'Avenues to it open wide:
'Tis done, my Wench, d'you nothing now perceive?
O dear HARRY! more than I could believe.
That dear enchanting Rod was surely made
To dig like Ground, by you of ADAM's trade,
And EVE herself, I warrant, work'd with such a Spade.

I am not suggesting that every seventeenth- or eighteenth-century book in the private case is so innocent or so 'normal'. But the British Museum subject indexes are not made for children. Why should their users not know about *News from Tybourn* (1677)? This execrably printed chapbook is 'An Account of the Confession and Execution of the Woman condemned for committing that horrid sin of Buggery with a Dog, which was also hanged on a Tree by her'. The dog, it is recorded, was only 'about ten inches high', and the woman steadfastly denied the offence.

Nevertheless she was hanged, and so was the little dog, amid the hostile exclamations of the spectators, and people paid a few coppers to read about it afterwards, just as they like to read about such goings on, real or imaginary, today. What is the point of keeping hidden from inquirers into Restoration manners and morals *The Duchess of Portsmouth's Garland*, twenty-five copies of which were printed in 1837 from a manuscript in the Faculty of Advocates' library, Edinburgh? This document gives a few poems and other pieces, in the manner of Rochester, attacking a lady ungallantly described as 'our Monarch's whore from France'. There is an interesting reference to 'new swindging dildoes, richly wrought/With satin and velvit ends', said to have been imported from France; and an even more interesting one to another importation: 'new fassion'd spunges to clear her twat/From slimy sperm and whites'. This is the earliest English reference to the vaginal sponge known to me, antedating by some fifty-five years the reference in Stretser's *New Description of Merryland*, and it is of some importance to the historian of contraceptive methods.

But zoöphilia, female auto-erotism, and contraceptive appliances are encountered comparatively rarely in the surviving sub-literature of these two centuries. Some information about deviant sexual behaviour in the eighteenth century may be obtained from the private case collection of trial reports: the seven volumes of *Trials for Adultery: or, the history of divorces* (1779–80), the two volumes of *The Cuckold's Chronicle* (1793), and so on; or from the semi-erotic magazines which retailed the sexual peccadillos of prominent men and women with undisguised relish. The five volumes of *The Bon Ton Magazine* (1792–95 [1791–96]), for instance, seem unknown to most social

76

historians, and the reader of the present book will have little difficulty in guessing why. Another neglected source is *Harris's List of Covent-Garden Ladies: or, man of pleasure's kalendar*, an annual listing the names (middle letters omitted), addresses, charges, peculiarities, and specialities of a large number of whores, rather as the ill-fated *Ladies Directory* [1959–60] did more recently. The private case has *Harris's List* for 1788–90 and 1793.

The greater part of this literature however is occupied with straightforward copulation and its attendant circumstances. Especially seduction, for accounts of which there seems to have been a wide audience of both sexes. The approach is generally humorous, a common theme being private lechery by persons who profess high principles. Quakers come in for more than their fair share of lampoons. In *A Merry Conversation which lately pass'd between a very noted Quaker, and his Maid, upon a very merry occasion* (3rd edn, 1739), John, the master, asks: 'Dost thou feel nothing *Mary*?' 'Yea,' says his maidservant, 'I feel something stiff against my Belly, as it were the Horn of a Unicorn.' 'My Undefiled,' says John, 'speak not of Unicorns, for there is nothing of the Beast between these Sheets: This is that Part of Carnal Man which riseth and falleth according to the Spirit within.' At length he tells her to spread one thigh towards the north, the other towards the south, and he will 'enter with Courage and Resolution, *and beat down* Satan *before me*'. When they have finished, Mary asks: 'When will the Spirit move thee again, Friend *John*?' and he replies: 'I will seek the *Laud*, and he will give us many Opportunities.' Seduction of a manservant by his mistress was a no less popular theme. In *Drive on Coachman* (1739), said to have been 'occasion'd by an affair lately discover'd in a family of quality', old and impotent Sir John, 'his Cuckold-Peepers open'd wide' by what he sees, encourages his coachman to fuck her ladyship: 'Since my Lady wants a Son;/I know she'll have her Bus'ness done;/So!—welcome, *Robin,—Pray drive on.*' In *Kick him Jenny*, eleven editions of which had appeared by 1737, another Sir John encourages Roger, 'a jolly country swain', to fuck Jenny, her ladyship's waiting-maid, while her ladyship, spying disapprovingly through another peep-hole, tells Jenny to 'kick him':

> Mad at his Wife, he cou'd have struck her,
> Aloud cry'd, —— her, *Roger*, —— her.
> Kick him, as loud the Dame went on;
> —— her, still louder, cry'd Sir *John*.

The dashes appear in the original. This little book is of interest in showing knowledge, and presumably use, of a coital posture supposedly inapt for conception:

> Thus in a Chair the cautious Dame,
> Who loves a little of That Same,
> Will take it on her Lover's Lap,
> Sure to prevent, this way, Mishap:
> Subtle Lechers! knowing that,
> They cannot so be got with Brat.

The group of eighteenth-century jest-books in the private case is of limited interest to all but specialists, and much inferior to the *Liber facetiarum* (written 1451, first published *c.* 1470) of Poggio Bracciolini (1380–1459) and the *Prouerbij . . . in facetie* ([Venice], 1525) of his countryman Antonio Cornazano (1429–84), English translations of which appeared in 1879 and 1888 respectively and are both in the private case. The English jokes are too obvious to raise more than a smile nowadays, though many of them can be traced back for centuries. Here are two specimens, both relying on paronomasia, from 'Roger Ranger, Gent.', *The Covent Garden Jester* (1785):

A music master teaching Lady L——r, a piece of music of his own composing, they came to a note with a dot, which makes any note where it is placed half as long again; this not being fully intelligible, occasioned the lady to miss her time, which the other observing says, 'madam, you have forgotten the prick.' 'Lord, sir, I did not see it.' 'I beg pardon, madam,' says the music master, 'I see my prick is too small.' The lady merrily said, 'Never mind it sir, let me put my hand to it, I will soon make it bigger.'

Dr. R——, who was not the humblest man in the world, being sent for by the late duke of Devon——, who was said to be one of the proudest, the duke received him while he was dressing his feet, and picking his toes, being at that time troubled with a diabetes; and upon the doctor's entering the room, accosted him in this manner, 'So, quack,' said he, 'I'm a dead man, for I piss sweet?' 'Do you,' replied the doctor, 'then prithee piss upon your toes, for they stink damnably', and so turning round on his heel, went out of the room.

Which brings us to scatology and the study of cloacal graffiti. The private case has a copy, wanting the fourth and final part, of that pioneering survey *The Merry-Thought: or, the glass-window and bog-house miscellany* [*c.* 1750]. Here are all kinds of verses scratched on windows and looking-glasses, and written on privy walls, with the provenance given of each. The standard of wit displayed in such inscriptions seems to have diminished over two centuries. Here is an example from 'a bog-house at the Nag's-Head in Bradmere':

> Such Places as these,
> Were made for the Ease
> Of every Fellow in common;
> But a Person who writes
> On the Wall as he sh-tes,
> Has a Pleasure far greater than Woman.
> For he's eased in his Body, and pleas'd in his Mind,
> When he leaves both a T——d and some Verses behind.

Under which was written, by a later visitor:

> You are eas'd in your Body, and pleas'd in your Mind
> That you leave both a T——d and some Verses behind;
> But to me, which is worse, I can't tell, on my Word,
> The reading your Verses, or smelling your T——d.

Outstanding among eighteenth-century erotica in the private case (leaving aside *Fanny Hill*) is *The History of the Human Heart; or, the adventures of a young gentleman.* Originally published in 1769 and reprinted in 1885 (the BM edition), it has been overshadowed by Cleland's novel and is crying out to be reprinted again by some enterprising publisher. He would not run into the same kind of difficulties as recent publishers of Cleland, for the anonymous *History of the Human Heart* is only partly devoted to descriptions of venery. It gives a vivid picture of mid-eighteenth-century low life in London and Holland; it is written with something of the gusto and tempo and detail of Defoe. It is a neglected minor masterpiece of the picaresque—one of the few private case books in English which can be read a second time for pleasure.

The History of the Human Heart tells the story of Camillo from fourteen hours before conception, when he was only a homunculus in his father's scrotum, to one hour after marriage, by which time his rakehelly days are over. His innocence is lost when he looks up his sister's petticoats as she stands, legs apart, in a cherry tree; his virginity, when a cousin 'bred at a Boarding School', where she learned 'vicious Tricks', succeeds in snapping his frenum, to his 'extreme Anguish'. A new and irresponsible tutor takes Camillo to London, where he has numerous adventures in brothels and elsewhere. We are introduced to the eighteenth-century equivalent of strip-tease: an exhibition performed by 'Posture Girls', one of whom tells her history, with which the company are 'mightily pleased'. The revellers resolve to spend the rest of the night 'by lying in State, that is each with a Brace of Girls'. Camillo however, though he 'liked a Girl well enough, . . . found no great Stomach for two or three at a time; and had so much Country Bashfulness left, that he scarce knew how to behave between them'. However, 'their busy Fingers were officiously employed to raise the pendent Member', and at last 'the heat of Blood got the better of his Embarassment'. One of the young women the hero meets is a Quaker, to whom he lays siege and whom he eventually fucks, after many frustrations, including a night with her maid who, in the dark, pretends to be the mistress. In Amsterdam he visits a brothel whose inmates spur his choice by giving him an apple and dancing round him naked, 'directing him to give the Apple to the happy She whom he most favoured' and putting themselves 'into all the antick Postures they could, as if to engage his Attention'. At this point the house is raided by the magistrates —or so Camillo is told—and he is pushed out, naked, into the cold at two in the morning. Beaten with a broomstick by the respectable citizens who find him, he is clapped into 'a stinking Dungeon, where he lay, cold and bruised, on a Wad of rotten Straw, and where a Million of Fleas lived at free Quarters on his defenceless Body'. This and other mishaps do not appreciably diminish his appetites. What does, inevitably, is marriage, to a young woman he seduces in Holland and deserts, but who follows him back to London:

> *Angelina* tempered Love, and the conjugal Bed with so much Discretion, that she perfectly reclaim'd the once wild *Camillo*, and made him own, that one Hour's Happiness with her, was worth an Age of those guilty Scenes, which he had spent so much Money, Time, and Youth, in the Pursuit of.

VI

EROTIC CLASSICS AND
AUTOBIOGRAPHIES

By 'CLASSICS' I mean erotica which have a certain degree
of literary merit, in that their intention is not solely to
arouse sexual excitement and their interest does not lie
solely in their descriptions of sexual activity. Soho book-
sellers interpret the word more broadly; if you mention,
say, *The Romance of Lust* (1873–76) to them they will
direct you to an antiquarian bookshop. For writings which
are essentially transcribed masturbation fantasies I have
borrowed the label 'hard-core pornography'. The border-
line is difficult to define, and the existence of erotic writings which are, or purport to be, autobiographical compli-
cates the distinction. 'The criterion', suggests Dr E. J.
Dingwall, honorary curator of the British Museum's private
case, 'is whether the work affords aesthetic satisfaction as
a whole, not merely sensual stimulation. . . . A piece of
writing which only stimulates sensual interest or desire and
does not afford aesthetic satisfaction as a whole is of medical,
psychological and anthropological interest rather than
literary.'

Generally speaking, the erotic classics retain some link
with reality. They reflect social conditions, manners, and

moral outlooks to some extent. They are not altogether devoid of plot, characterization, or humour; or, in periods when sex manuals and marriage guidance are unknown, they may have some didactic purpose. For all that, they may depict scenes no less lubricious than are to be found in some of the 'hard-core' publications.

I have already hinted at the scarcity of erotic classics in English. There are many in French. I am not sure why this difference exists, but I suspect it has something to do with the way sex was driven out of the English novel in the latter half of the eighteenth century. The castration of English imaginative literature made the English clandestine literature of sex the most poverty-stricken and boring in Europe. The one obvious exception, John Cleland's *Memoirs of a Woman of Pleasure* (1749 [1748–49]), commonly known as *Fanny Hill*, was published before the literary dissociation of the erotic from the rest of life had really begun. The BM private case has twelve separate editions, including the first, of the one English erotic classic known, at least by repute, to everybody.

I have not read *The Memoirs of a Voluptuary* (1905), which Dawes praised so highly, and there is no copy in the BM. There is however another English erotic novel in the private case which seems to me to have some literary merit (though, unlike *Fanny Hill*, it uses the frankest language for sex organs and sexual activity). This is *Vénus* [sic] *in India or love adventures in Hindustan* (Brussels, 1889) by 'Captain C. Deveureux, of the General Staff'. The scenes it depicts never exceed the limits of the possible or, indeed, the probable, and many episodes in the life of a British army officer in India have the ring of truth about them. There is nothing inherently unbelievable in the earthy and generously disposed woman, an NCO's wife, who makes herself available to the hero without much persuasion and teaches him, among other things, 'heel and toe':

> 'Beginning each stroke from the very beginning and ending it with the very end. . . . You *almost* pull it out, but not quite, and never stop short in your thrust, but send your prick *home*, with a sharp rap of your balls against my bottom! and that's what is *good*!' And she appeared to smack her lips involuntarily.

There is a brilliant account of the attempted rape of a sixteen-year-old English girl by an Afghan, who escapes when the narrator surprises him at the moment of ejaculation. 'The incredible insolence, which could have animated a *Native* of any kind, in time of peace and in our own borders, to commit such a crime, astounded me', comments 'Captain Deveureux'. But Fanny Selwyn has not been penetrated, and the blood the narrator sees is menstrual. Meanwhile a second Afghan has been quietly buggering Fanny's sister Amy, and 'Captain Deveureux' kills him, thus making himself the hero of the Selwyn family. In due course he takes the maidenheads of Fanny and Amy—whom he arouses by telling them the detailed story of his wedding night—and of their younger but rather more passionate sister Mabel. What distinguishes *Vénus in India* from the great mass of hard-core pornography in English which was appearing in the latter half of the last century, and continued to appear until about 1910, is its credibility. The women in it are not merely projections of the author's inflamed imagination. The characters as a whole are not simply male and female sex organs in various permutations, but human beings interested in finding satisfactory sexual partners.

English translations of some of the foreign erotic classics

can be consulted at the BM; they are not always reliable, and those students who can read the originals had better do so. One translation which can however be recommended unreservedly is the *Index expurgatorius* (1868) of the Spanish-born poet Marcus Valerius Martialis (A.D. 40–104), usually called Martial. When an English version of his epigrams appeared in 1860, in Bohn's Classical Library, the more obscene, which are not the least instructive about Roman social life of that period, were left in the original Latin (though an Italian rendering by the eighteenth-century lexicographer Giuspanio Graglia was appended to each of the untranslated epigrams). A group of friends, among them the journalist and novelist George Augustus Sala (1828–96) and the pornographer Captain Edward Sellon (1818–66), decided to produce an English version of what had been omitted. They printed the fruits of their labours in an edition of 150 copies. Each epigram has a literal prose translation, a verse translation, and notes. The introduction hits out at the 'superficial morality among the English of the present day' and at the 'monomania for refining impurities' which pervaded every English work then written on Greece or Rome. Martial's cynicism is well conveyed in this translation of the twenty-ninth epigram of book XI, 'To Phyllis':

Oh, if ought of stiffness lingers,
The palsied touch of those wan fingers
Kills me outright, and but an hour's
Exposure to the withering showers
Of 'ducks' and 'darlings' pouring from your tongue
Leaves what you love for half a day unstrung;
Phyllis, you know not how to seize
The happy knack to win and please;

Bid me accept your house in town,
Your country seat, ten thousand down;
Forget your fingers, open wide your hand,
For that's the way to make your Martial stand.

The sixty-third epigram of the same book, 'To Philomusus',
deals wittily with an everyday aspect of Roman life:

> Philomusus, oft you eye us
>   In the bath, and then ask why
> Handsome, well hung slaves are by us,
>   Dress, undress and rub us dry.
> This answer, prying friend, I give,
> They bugger the inquisitive.

A common medium for sexual instruction—notably,
instruction in coital and other erotic techniques—in the
sixteenth and seventeenth centuries was a dialogue between
an older, experienced woman and a young, inexperienced
relative. The baffling histories of the four chief works of
this kind were unravelled by Mr David Foxon, at that
time a BM official, in an erudite series of articles for *The
Book Collector*, 1963, conveniently reprinted as *Libertine
Literature in England 1660–1745* (1964). Aretino's *Ragionamenti* seem to have stimulated his secretary Niccolò
Franco to produce *La Puttane Errante* [*c.* 1650], which in
turn was imitated, probably by Michel Millot, in *L'Escole
des filles* (Paris, 1655). This was the book that Pepys,
having drunk 'mighty good store of wine', read 'for
information sake' one Sunday, burning it afterwards 'that
it might not be among my books to my shame'. The private
case has a beautiful copy of the 1668 edition, printed in
Holland. There is no English translation extant. The book
is a 'Collection of the principal things you should know in

order to make your husbands happy when you have them', and it is written simply, charmingly, and with constant emphasis on physical pleasure and other important details so often omitted from present-day manuals:

> When a lad loves a girl he says, 'Do you love me?' and if the girl says yes . . . he raises her shift and opens her legs while he unties his own clothing, and when he has done so he lies on her belly and, into the hole out of which she pisses, he stuffs that long engine with the greatest pleasure and delight in the world. . . .
> How can that be done when it is so soft and flabby?
> It is not always so soft—it grows longer, it becomes hard and stiff as a rod.

The last of these four dialogues is Nicolas Chorier's *Aloisiae Sigeae Toletanae Satyra Sotadica de arcanis Amoris et Veneris* [c. 1660], which purports to be a translation of a work by a Spanish lady. There are no fewer than thirty-eight copies of various editions and translations in the private case. The intention of this book is patently less straightforward than those of its predecessors, and it is not to everyone's taste. There is a sadistic vein in it, and an emphasis on defloration:

> When Caviceo had ascended, a furious fit of lust came over me. I began to hug him, to entice him by my looks, to excite him by my sighs; he too commenced to smack me sweetly, to toy with my nether mouth, to play his fingers in the moss and between the lips. I suddenly feel a very delicious flood issuing from my veins, rushing in an impetuous course out of the cisterns of the womb, augmented by that humor with which he had drenched me. . . . 'Now', said he, 'I want thee,

darling, to count all my bounces. . . .' . . . And while my thoughts are busy in counting, he impetuously broke my door open and plunged the furious mentule up to the dangling-bobs into the sanctuary of Venus. A very smart pain forced me to shout. . . . 'Thou hast already passed through the worst part of it', said he, 'behold, my joy, thou hast taken the whole of me in, however long and thick I am.'

The greatest writer of erotic romances is, in my opinion, André-Robert Andréa de Nerciat (1739–1800), whose works are a storehouse of arcane information about the tastes, habits, fantasies, and appliances of different social classes. The private case has four editions of *Les Aphrodites* (Lampsaque, 1793); five of *Mon Noviciat* ([Berlin], 1792); eleven of *Félicia ou mes fredaines* ('Londres' [i.e. Paris], 1775); and three of what I find most remarkable of all, the posthumously published *Le Diable au corps*, written about 1788 and first printed in Mézières in 1803. A thousand copies of the first edition were seized on arrival in Paris. The characters in this libertine romance include lords and ladies, servants, monks, other ecclesiastics, a donkey that brays with post-coital joy, and a seller of condoms and dildoes who has been denounced by two un-grateful nuns to whom he sold a double dildo. This merchant discusses his wares with a marquise, arouses her, and falls on her, at which point an abbé who has been hiding in the wardrobe rushes out saying 'Good morning, all!', joins in the fun, *per anum*, and returns to his hiding-place with the words: 'Another convert!' The scene with the donkey ('A donkey, in one's home! what a treasure!' says a comtesse enviously) is, to my mind, the funniest in erotic literature. For Andréa de Nerciat in English, one must turn to Dugdale's obscure periodical *The Exquisite* [1842–44], where there are some translations by James Campbell Reddie, or to a free rendering of *La Matinée libertine* ('Cythère', 1787), entitled *The Marchioness's Amorous Pastimes and some other merry tales* ('London' [i.e. Brussels], 1893). One of the merry tales relates the experience of a male guest who is using a 'night-chair' in the dark when a woman enters without observing him, lifts her petticoats, sits on his lap, and proceeds to urinate.

In small doses, *L'Anti-Justine* (Paris, 1798) by Nicolas-Anne-Edme Restif de la Bretonne (1734–1806) is almost as entertaining. It is translated by 'Pieralessandro Casavini' (i.e. Austryn Wainhouse) as *Pleasures and Follies of a Good-Natured Libertine* (Paris, 1955), and this is in the private case, too. It is a rollicking but far too lengthy satire on Sade's *Justine* (1791), mercifully without the flagellation. There is virtually everything else, including cannibalism, wife-lending, and two of Restif's obsessions: incest and shoe- and foot-fetichism. Restif intended *L'Anti-Justine*, or so he claimed, 'to awaken amorous sentiments in gentlemen whose ladies presently inspire none in them', and promised that 'the reading of but one chapter must be enough to move a man to the proper exploitation of his wife, young or old, pretty or ill-favored, provided the lady have an hygienic acquaintance with the bidet and a well-developed taste in footwear'. Its effect is rather to arouse laughter.

The same effect, unless the reader is devoutly religious, is produced by the anti-clerical tales which form a noteworthy sub-division of the erotic classics. Jean-Charles Gervaise de Latouche (c. 1715–82) wrote one of the liveliest: *Histoire de Dom B******, *portier des Chartreux*, first published before 1745. Similar, but cruder, is *Le Tartufe libertin* ('Cythère' [i.e. Paris, c. 1831]), whose hero persuades the

Lady Superior of a girls' orphanage to corrupt her charges while he watches from an armchair. Coarse though they are, these tales rank above a number of pedestrian English imitations, including *Nunnery Tales* [Paris? *c.* 1888] and *The Autobiography of a Flea* ('1789' [1889]).

Human authors, too, have written erotic autobiographies; certain editions of some of the more famous remain in the private case. With Casanova, it is clearly because of the obscene illustrations in the twelve-volume Nichols-Smithers-Robson-Karslake edition of 1894. There are 101 of them —two have been ripped from the BM set—designed by Jean-Adolph Chauvet about the year 1875. (The originals, incidentally, were bound in a set of Casanova in French which was seized from an American naval officer by the US Customs soon after the war and is now in the Library of Congress.) It is not generally realized that the translation of the first half of this edition, though later reprinted as Arthur Machen's alone, is a word-for-word plagiarism by Machen of the 'A. Tolliab' (i.e. A. Baillot) translation, published in Brunswick in 1863. Frank Harris seems nearly as well represented in the private case as on the bookstalls. Thanks to Dawes, the BM now has a copy of the first volume of the first edition of *My Life and Loves* (Paris, 1922). And there are editions of various autobiographical writings by Henry Miller, including the revised version (Paris, 1957) of his little-known *The World of Sex*.

But these three autobiographers are all now in paperback and sold legally. How long will it be before they are joined by that mammoth among sexual autobiographies, or sexual diaries, the legendary *My Secret Life* ('Amsterdam' [i.e. Brussels? *c.* 1888–94])? In these eleven volumes, the last half-volume being taken up with a 46-page table of contents and an 87-page subject index, a nineteenth-century English gentleman describes his sex life, from childhood to late middle age, in copious detail and with the utmost frankness. The author's identity is unknown, though Mr Gershon Legman makes out a case for identifying him as H. S. Ashbee. The author is not concerned to rationalize his behaviour. He provides 'a plain narrative of facts and not a psychological analysis'. The result is a text of fascinating and often harrowing authenticity. That truth is here eked out with fantasy is more than likely. But in essentials this flatly written record forces acceptance by its sheer mass of detail. And not only erotic detail. What work of imaginative pornography admits fleas, crab-lice, venereal diseases, alcoholism, poverty, dirt, the stinks and sores of Victorian London? *My Secret Life* teems with just such details, whose effect is to stimulate compassion, not desire:

The women in the streets I have described had fine women among them, but for the most part they were plain in face, indifferent in form somewhere, and hideously coarse in manner; but the beauty of this woman was so great, I forgot all her coarseness. When I came to myself after my pleasures, she was fast asleep. She had perhaps spent, that and the liquor called gin overpowered her, and she forgot her business. Then the biting of fleas worried me for half-an-hour. I spent my time in hunting for them and scratching myself, snuffing with my fingers the only tallow candle, and now and then holding it over her to look at her beautiful face, naked body, and unwashed cunt. The heat was intolerable. . . .

Whether the slight dozing had relieved her brain, or whether the fumes of the liquor had evaporated, I don't know, but she soon became more conscious, and, though stupid, yet more wide awake. Her voice still had the thick utterance, her answers were still those of a person only partly understanding what was said to her. I expect I had excited her passions by my fingers, and not by what I said, for after awaking she again blurted out, 'Fuck me—I want a fuck.' A grab at my prick showed that she knew where to find the means of giving herself pleasure, and I gave it her. Then I dozed.

Knocks at the door aroused me, and a shrill voice cried out, 'Kate, Kate.' I listened. 'Are you alone?' said the voice. I shook Kate, and awakened her a little. 'Someone is knocking at your door', said I. 'Oh! damn—arseholes', said she, turning on her side and dozing again.

'Kate'—knock, knock—'Kate, are you alone? I'm going to bolt the door—they are all in', said the voice.

Kate made no reply. I was dressing, so opened the door. 'I'm here, and I am going directly.' 'Is she drunk?' said the woman. 'I think she is.' 'Do you know her?' 'No.' 'Well, I will leave the door open.' 'I'm going—wait.' There lay Kate dozing. When dressed, I said, 'I have left five shillings on the table.' 'Awake her', said the woman (for I heard and saw it was one). 'You had better.' 'Kate, Kate', sang out the woman. I shook Kate, who turned, opened her eyes, and said, 'Oh! damn—don't.' 'Come in', said I to the woman. She did, and shook Kate. 'Oh! arseholes', said Kate, and again closed her eyes. 'She's been lushing for three days', said the woman. 'Mind there are five shillings', said I, and disgusted I left, resolving never to go near the drunken beast again.

He does however, a few days later.

A single extract cannot do more than suggest the flavour of *My Secret Life*, which is in many ways the strangest book in the private case.* Only a policeman could mistake it for the sort of writing which is the subject of the next chapter.

* Professor Steven Marcus devotes two chapters of *The Other Victorians* (1966) to *My Secret Life,* and my own abridgement of it is shortly to appear.

VII

HARD-CORE PORNOGRAPHY

THE WRITER of real pornography is aiming, in Sir Alan
Herbert's vivid and truthful phrase, to make the reader as
randy as possible as often as possible. The reader is seeking a
substitute for sexual experience, or for sexual experience of a
certain kind which he may be unable, or unwilling, to
secure. This sub-literature whose intention is to arouse the
sexual appetite remains less acceptable to society than the
sub-literature whose themes are violence and murder. A
detailed account of a bullet in a woman's belly—what it
does, what it feels like, how her body reacts, how blood
spurts out, how she screams and writhes in agony—is emi-
nently publishable and accessible both to children and to
the minority who find it sexually exciting. So detailed a
description of sexual pleasure is taboo. Dons write gruesome
murder stories under their own names and keep their jobs;
pornographers, however eminent, must use pseudonyms
and publish clandestinely. Libraries and bookshops display
books which make your blood run cold; but not books
meant to make it hot.

This state of affairs has unfortunate results for pornography and for its public, which is much wider than Mr
Robert Pitman and Mrs Mary Whitehouse would have us
believe. Readers will accept, devour, and get steamed up

over lamentably ill-written productions. Just as hungry men slaver over any kind of cookery book, sexually hungry men pay incredibly high prices for books consisting of lavatory wall fantasies cobbled together without any pretence at literary skill. There are levels of squalor in this part of the private case, down to the grimly apolaustic illiteracy of *Moslem Erotism* [printed Holland or Germany? *c.* 1900?], *The Little People* [Paris? *c.* 1909], *Realistic Pleasures Gathered from the Diary of a Sybarite* [Paris? 1900?], which could just as well have been 'printed at Alexandria, 1900–1901', as its title-page claims, and my own favourite titles: *Lovely Nights of Young Grils* [sic] *Served Up Seasoned and Prepared for Amatory Feasts* [Paris, *c.* 1895?] and *The Lustful Memoirs of a Young and Passionated* [sic] *Girl* ('Paris and London', 1904). Yet even these specimens, apart from being unintentionally comical, are not without a certain scientific and historical interest. To quote the honorary curator of the private case once more:

In erotic and pornographic literature lies an almost untapped mine of information ... dealing with the most intimate and secret activities of mankind. For here we have a picture of human sexual activity that is provided by nothing else except perhaps in the confessions of patients or penitents, and of these, few ever see the light. Moreover not only can we see the actualities and fantasies of the sexual life laid bare, but we can compare these manifestations as they are described by different peoples in different ages and under different social conditions. Thus the effect of historical circumstances and cultural changes may be traced, the relation of erotic customs and habits to contemporary events made clear, and some sort of rough measurement attempted whereby the imagination and sophistication of the age can be gauged.

Since practically all hard-core pornography is written by men for men to read, its subject-matter provides a fairly reliable index of the predominant themes in male sexual fantasy at any given period. Leaving aside for separate consideration the specialist literatures of homosexuality and sado-masochism, it is clear that, for at least one hundred years, many heterosexual men in this country have cherished the image of a totally permissive woman. She is easily aroused; insatiable; always ready to take the initiative; expert at giving and receiving pleasure; generous with every orifice. She demands from her partners neither tenderness nor a lasting, or even responsible, relationship. This ideal playmate is woman remade with a male psychology, responding to the sort of psychological stimuli that men themselves react to. 'The kind men like', as the American advertisements say. In real life, such women are rare. In sex fantasy literature, minute descriptions of their erotic frenzies and multiple orgasms cover page after page. Even men who would run like hell from such a woman if they encountered her in the flesh find pleasure in reading about the exploits of a 'nymphomaniac'.

One of the most agreeable heroines of this kind is the eponymous narrator of *The Modern Eveline: or the adventures of a young lady of quality who was never found out* (Paris, 1904), an unusually well-written fantasy in three volumes, purporting to be a modernization of an earlier book. Eveline is a baronet's daughter who cannot say no—except to clergymen, at whom she draws the line. Taught fellatio by a hunchback ('I revelled in my discovery of the male organ in all its strength and virility'), she is

97

attracted, at seventeen, to a footman whom she thinks 'magnificent in his handsome livery, with his gold garters, black silk stockings, and his crimson plush breeches'. She tells him to take her boots off and rub her sore ankle, while she rubs her foot on those plush breeches: ' "What have you got in your pocket, John? Is it a flute?" "No, miss, I am not musical. I don't play any instrument." The man blushed scarlet as his breeches, and seemed quite confused. "It feels exactly like one, John, and it gets bigger and bigger." ' Before investigating further however, this astonishingly advanced young lady of quality goes to a Soho chemist's to buy a contraceptive syringe ('There are some things one must do for oneself') and loses her virginity to the young man who serves her. Then back to the footman, who is soon re-aroused:

> It stuck up in front of him like a great peg to hang dresses on.
> 'What a beauty he looks, John!'
> 'He is that, miss. My mother first found that out when I was a little 'un, miss. She used to show him to the neighbours. One old single lady used to bring him biscuits.'
> 'Biscuits—John—why? How could he swallow biscuits?'
> 'I ate 'em for him, miss. They went down to him that way, I suppose. They was gingerbread nuts, miss. Anyhow he got fine and large.'

Eveline gives herself to an exhibitionist; to a police inspector who uses cold cream ('the best in the whole world—from Bond Street') as a lubricant; to her German music master (more fellatio: he shouts, *Mein Gott in Himmel! I go off! I come on! Ach! Ach! Ach!*'); to a young sailor on leave after ten months at sea ('He could see at times up to my knee. . . . He was evidently getting excited': how times have changed!); to a man she meets on a train; to her bootmaker, who tongues her 'with all the fury of a satyr'; to her brother and father; and to an assortment of policemen and servants, including Jim the groom:

> 'Would you like to have a bit of fun with me, Jim?'
> 'Oh, miss, that would not be for the likes of me! You are such a beautiful young lady—so thorough-bred.'
> 'You may play with me if you like, Jim.'

Eveline soon reaches the simple conclusion that 'there is no pleasure for a woman equal to the delight of witnessing the sexual transports of which she is the cause'. Accordingly, to save time, she ceases to wear drawers: 'I hate drawers. I hate all which troubles my pleasure.'

The same short way with the servant problem is found in *Clara Alcock: her initiation in the ways of love and full enjoyment of its sweets* ('Glasgow, 1898' [i.e. Paris, 1911?]) by 'Lord Ferrars', in which Lady Flora, to whom coition is 'the most delightful sensation in the world', practises it with Tomkins the butler. Meanwhile Madden, a labourer, 'a fine burly-looking fellow, the very picture of manly strength and good temper', between whose legs is 'an unusually large protuberance', is satisfying Lady Flora's niece Clara Alcock and Susan, her ladyship's maid. After which Lady Flora takes Susan's place by stealth, standing on a seat in the summer-house and sticking her bottom out through a convenient opening. Aimée, in *The Small Rooms of Paris* (Paris, 1956) by 'Ezra de Richarnaud', enjoys on occasion three lovers in as many hours and arranges it so that they never meet: ' "Sometimes I have

99

one leaving by the stairs while another is arriving by the elevator." "You've got hot pants", I teased, feeling a little hot myself. "That's right. Howabout you getting into them?" ' But the man who is keeping her arrives inopportunely and the narrator has to spend three hours hidden in the bathtub with a leaking tap dripping on his forehead. Another lady in the same book, Elena, has twenty-six sex-starved sailors one after another. A third, Irma, manages thirty. The motives for such permissiveness are rarely made clear; but there is an agreeable, if momentary, touch of realism in *Sheaves from an Old Escritoire* ('London' [i.e. Paris or Brussels], 1896), which is set in an Eastbourne school for young ladies: ' "Oh!" cried Lucy, "he's going to try and poke me, as John did last week, and I have hardly been able to move since!" "Let him have you," Norah cried, "if John has done it, or we shall get no peace." '

The fantasy woman takes great delight in the use of obscene language to excite herself and her lovers, a predilection known technically as erotolalia. Frequently her excited cries have a masochistic flavour. In *A Town-Bull or the Elysian fields* ('New Orleans' [i.e. Brussels], 1893), Mrs Belle Seaton, a New York lady who debauches her confessor with ease, cries: 'See me, a sensual slave to all the lust you can pour into me. . . . Talk bawdy, vulgarly, wildly, lecherously, teach me all you know of lustful pleasure. Even the most outré. Order me around as you would a common strumpet.' And later: 'I am your slave, your whore, your harlot, ready to be whored out in the public streets, if you want to. I only live to be whored. I will die for it!' Towards the sexual climax, the language tends to disintegrate. Aimée, in *The Small Rooms of Paris*, yells as she comes: 'Gee-beetch, wee-acha. Bubu nof. Ug-slip plifzee. Ahaaa!' How successful this is, each reader must judge for himself.

When the fantasy woman is not making noises of this kind, it is generally because she has a penis in her mouth. But fear of castration occasionally breaks through the fellatio fantasy, as in *Abandon* (Paris, 1958) by 'B. von Soda', where Yvonne, imprisoned and unco-operative, bites off a psychiatrist's penis, thus earning the admiration of the tough female prisoners who have hitherto persecuted her: 'Nobody's goin' bother ya if ya don't wanna be bothered, you a cock-biting bitch-blonde and we're all for ya.'

Outside pornography the dildo is, I believe, rather uncommon; but the fantasy woman always seems to have one to hand, using it with gusto to entertain both herself and her friends of either sex. Some are elaborate affairs; the one in *Sheaves from an Old Escritoire*, for instance, squirts 'jets of perfumed water'.

Very often the fantasy woman has a daughter, and the hero demonstrates his prowess by seducing, or being seduced by, both in turn. Or even simultaneously. This mother-daughter seduction fantasy is the theme of one of the most remarkable twentieth-century French erotic novels, *Trois filles de leur mère* [1926] by 'Pierre Louÿs' (i.e. Pierre Louis, 1870–1925), translated into English by Richard Seaver and Norman Rubington as *The She-Devils* (Paris, 1958). Much inferior is *A Nocturnal Meeting* [Paris? *c.* 1909–10] by 'Ramrod', the first of two volumes issued under the general title of *My Lustful Adventures*. It concludes:

Many a thundering good grind I have had from those two amiable women since. I frequently meet them in society. . . . Whenever I see their bare shoulders at dinner or ball, and note the admiration they inspire,

I secretly chuckle to think how often I have stripped them still barer, and wantoned over the hills and dales of both those female forms divine.

Very often, too, the fantasy woman is pretty clearly a mother figure. She may be disguised, thinly, as an aunt. But there are books where the mother-son incest taboo is set aside. The father-daughter one, too. Incest is carried to extreme and ridiculous lengths in *The Romance of Lust* (1873–76) by William S. Potter and others. After a long (four volumes) and boring series of incestuous orgies, Count Ferdinando crowns the tale by telling of his incestuous union with his sister who is also his daughter, and of his subsequent enjoyment of the daughter of this union.

Most of the hard-core books include at least one scene of group sexual activity, which may be quite mild and amusing, as in *Maudie: revelations of life in London* (1909). Like Eveline, Maudie attracts men's attention by 'showing her lovely legs right up to the knee'. She undoes men's fly buttons with her teeth (what would she have done with zips?). And she tells them: 'You look like a submarine with the periscope stuck out of the water.' She is an adept at the 'kangaroo fuck', where the woman jumps on the man's erect penis and he catches her under the armpits. At one point the hero

was just going to sleep when the door opened very quietly, and *another* girl came into the moonlight. . . . The original giggled in the sheets. 'You don't mind May, do you?' she said. 'No', was Charlie's answer; 'but it's got to stop at May, you and May. If I've got to go through the whole *personnel* of the establishment, I give up.'

Other orgies are more enterprising and more complex. *Unfaithful* (Paris, 1960) by 'Peter Jason' goes fairly systematically through various combinations, including the 'sex swastika', or double sixty-nine. Riva, a Turkish girl, after five (or is it six?) ordinary orgasms in a row, has the greatest of her entire sexual career when two men enjoy her simultaneously, one in the vagina, the other in the rectum. The characters in the same author's *Wayward* (Paris, 1961) are even more versatile, to the point where our credulity is a trifle strained when twenty couples, watching a secretly shot film of their previous orgy, achieve staggering new combinations, while

> on the face of the baroness de Bierli, buried beneath the lascivious mass of her fuckers, played a beatific, Mona Lisa smile. It was the smile of triumph of the scientist in the moment of discovery, the smile of the athlete who has broken an Olympian record.

After this, the group activity in *The Small Rooms of Paris*, where mustard is licked off a penis, champagne is poured on breasts, and oysters and ketchup are sucked out of a vagina, is pretty small beer.

Complementing the permissive, experienced woman portrayed in these fantasies is the unwilling or inexperienced woman, frequently a virgin, who has to be initiated, seduced, deflowered, or raped. Initiation is the theme of *The Simple Tale of Suzan Aked*, first published in Brussels in 1891, in which occur quaint echoes of the *Ragionamenti* type of dialogue:

> 'Have you never read any novels, nor any love stories, Susan?'
> 'No! my father and mother said they were foolish stuff.'

'I have heard them say so. And have you not even Sir Walter Scott or Shakespeare in the house?'

'Shakespeare we have, I know; but it is locked up in papa's study, in the glass bookcase. I have never read it.'

'Ah! then read *Romeo and Juliet* and you may perhaps learn a secret or two.'

Lucia, the initiator, finds that Susan wears unsuitable drawers:

'Why! they are only cut up behind. You ought to have them cut up to the waistband in front too, Susan.'

'Why?'

'Because how on earth could your lover feel you if you had things like this on? . . . And how on earth could you manage an *al fresco* poke if you wore these drawers?'

So Lucia runs to the dressing table, takes a pair of scissors, and, 'before I knew what she was at, she had the point through the calico and ripped it down'. Susan hears about the coital posture known as the 'nutcrackers', and receives much biological and contraceptive information. 'A man's spend', she is told, 'literally swarms with spermatozoids . . . something like tadpoles in shape'—and Lucia describes how she saw them under the microscope, thanks to the generosity of Charlie—nineties pornography 'literally swarms' with Charlies—who fucks three girls one after another in order to provide specimens. In the third specimen, though, the 'dangerous little tadpoles' were 'all dead as door nails'.

Defloration is sometimes presented as agreeable for the female, as in *The Corpse Wore Grey* (Paris, 1962) by 'Peter O'Neill', where Ellen says: 'You're the first man

that's ever made me feel that I want to lose my virginity.'
The feeling is as short-lived as the virginity. 'It was like
going to the moon', says Ellen. More frequently, however,
the less agreeable sides of the process are stressed or, as in
the many books of 'Marcus van Heller' (i.e. John Cole-
man), there is obsessive emphasis on sexual violence. His
Adam and Eve (Paris, 1961) shows the transformation of
Eve from virgin to permissive fantasy woman. To get a
part in a play, she makes up to a theatrical agent, who
'whisks' her to 'an elegant bar', then 'flashes' her to his
flat in Maida Vale ('the area where the expensive prostitutes lived'). She changes her mind at the sight of his penis,
which resembles 'a cannon poking from a thicket under an
overhanging cliff'. Too late: 'there was a sudden deep,
thrusting entry as if a red-hot pole had been thrust into her
body'. The agent tells her thoughtfully: 'You're the first
virgin I've ever had.' He does it again, and she feels as sore
as if he had used a potato peeler. Meanwhile her friend
Adam, a 19-year-old solicitor's clerk who paints, is being
seduced by Mrs Gracie Goldenbaum, who whispers 'You
beautiful, beautiful boy' and is old enough to be his mother,
'but this simply added a perverse fascination to the whole
thing'. As she orders a post-coital meal, he thinks: 'This is
the life—the only life for me.' Eve's misfortunes continue:
soon she is being painfully buggered by another prospective
employer. Her next step up the ladder is a famous drama
critic ('How young he was, and handsome!'). This goes
rather better: 'It was a dream, a heavenly nightmare. . . .
She was a goddess and he was a god—the goddess of cunt
and the god of prick in a heavenly fuck.' Adam, alas! over-
hears this divine encounter and revenges himself on Eve by
raping her: 'You'll be treated like a whore. I hope you
choke with it.' Before long Adam falls in with members of

the British Society of Witches, who whip up excitement by prancing in a ring, naked, slashing at each other with switches; soon Adam is part of 'a knot of wriggled [sic], gasping bodies, a many-headed, many-armed monster with five voracious sexual organs'. Eve finds her road to stardom leads through the bed of Lady Celia. But having by now grown somewhat hardened to pain, she does not flinch from her ladyship's rubber dildo (' "I want to see you squirm and cry out in helpless passion" . . . "O dear god, dear god", she cried and, for some reason, tears came into her eyes. . . . It was like being impaled on a stake'). After Eve has been returning the compliment for three-quarters of an hour, in front of a looking-glass, her education is completed: a trapdoor opens in the ceiling and Lady Celia's husband peers down. 'Wonderful', he says. 'I've lived through every second of it.'

So, no doubt, has the reader, though this author's style, *mutatis mutandis*, would not disgrace a women's magazine of the old-fashioned sort. *Rape* (Paris, 1955), for instance, which shows him once again on top of his favourite subject, is full of phrases like 'the thin strip of silk hiding her vital citadel which I was all set to take by storm'.

A special sub-class of defloration fantasies is concerned with very young girls. The most famous of these is Captain Edward Sellon's *The New Epicurean* ('1740' [1865]), where the victims address their seducer as 'dear sir', are either impossibly knowing or impossibly ignorant, and play blind-man's buff, hunt the slipper, hide and seek, and swinging ('Oh! the dear little feet, the fucktious shoes, the racy delectable legs; nothing could be finer'). *Letters from a Friend in Paris* (1874) has a father deflowering his daughter at puberty. Of more general interest is the handful of books where a man's loss of virginity is described in some detail. *Maidenhead Stories* ('Chicago' [i.e. Brussels?], 1894) by 'John Smith' portrays the final supper of the Beta Theta Society at Smith College, where 'two of the handsomest and most shameless women of the town' have been engaged to make a man of 21-year-old Frank Eaton, an exceptionally shy student. To help awaken his interest, thirteen young men, and the two girls, tell the stories of their first sexual experience. It is a slight but amusing book, and ends with this generalization: 'In 99 cases out of 100 the untried youth is too timid, too shy to force his point to the conclusion, unless he is aided at the critical moment by woman's ready tact.'

Sometimes the fantasy seducer smooths his path with aphrodisiacs. James Campbell Reddie, in *The Amatory Experiences of a Surgeon* ('Moscow' [i.e. London], 1881), makes a curious reference to the external application of ginger for this purpose. In *Sixfold Sensuality or the sensual pleasure giving exercises of an ingenious acrobatic family* [Paris or Brussels? *c*. 1902] by 'A Cairene' (*acrobatic* on the title-page of this reprint being a mistake for *aristocratic*, though, as Dawes remarks, it serves equally well for a description), the wily seducer Adolph employs 'Cantharide'. He calls it 'stomach medicine', puts it in his port wine and lemonade, then switches drinks with his childhood friend Ella, who is a virgin. After half an hour Ella is flushed and her breathing is short, and Adolph slips his 'manufacturing machine' into her hand remarking that it has grown a little, has it not? since they were playmates together. Not to put too fine a point on it, Adolph displays 'a horn like a telegraph pole', and Ella loses her virginity before you can say 'GPO'. By now it is almost time for the theatre, and they get dressed, 'smacking each other all the time'. After the play they find supper laid for them in the 'Dinning room': cold turkey and mutton. They fall to, tickling each other and eating out of each other's mouths, and declaring 'it was the happiest day of their lives'.

This scene of innocent enjoyment seems as good a place as any to conclude our survey of the heterosexual fantasies preserved at the BM for future generations. But the reader who wants to exercise his right to sample one or two—and they are, after all, public property—might care to know my own personal choice. It is *Play This Love with Me* (Paris, 1955) by 'Willie Baron', a skit on the hard-boiled crime novel. This is not nearly so rubbishy as most of the hard-core stuff. In fact it is fun to read: especially the scene in which two friends share a lady whose vagina and mouth are singularly prehensile, while smoking *Cannabis indica* through a narghile and listening to cool jazz; and the hardly less hilarious take-off of a black mass. I hereby nominate this 'best buy', as it were, on the hard-core counter; and if you can convince the BM authorities you are a serious student, you should have an amusing couple of hours. Again, Mr George Steiner, otherwise a harsh critic of this form of entertainment, has admitted to finding at least one 'nugget' in 'Harriet Daimler' (i.e. Iris Owens), *The Woman Thing* (Paris, 1958); and who am I to disagree?

Incidentally, some of the other Olympia Press publications in the private case have no business there at all: *The Naked Lunch* (Paris, 1959) and *The Soft Machine* (Paris, 1961) by William Burroughs, for example, and *The Ticket That Exploded* (Paris, 1962), which Burroughs wrote in collaboration with Michael Portman. It is equally hard to understand why James Hanley's sensitive and utterly unstimulating novel *Boy* (1931), condemned thirty-two years ago in a very different climate of opinion, and in Manchester at that, should remain in the private case.

VIII

HOMOSEXUAL AND SADO-MASOCHISTIC LITERATURE

SOME OF the most interesting and best-written of the books in the private case form part of the extensive literature of male homosexuality. Many of these were locked away in a less enlightened age, when mere mention of this sexual preference was enough to render a book at least unrespectable. The Wilde trials in 1895 made it difficult for other writers besides Havelock Ellis to discuss homosexuality. Thus 'Xavier Mayne' (i.e. Edward I. P. Stevenson) had two books on the subject published in Naples. One is *Imre: a memorandum* (1906), a restrained and decent tale about a friendship between an Englishman and a young Hungarian officer. The other is *The Intersexes: a history of similisexualism as a problem in social life* [*c.* 1910], an undeservedly neglected study filled with fascinating information on, for example, male prostitution and blackmail. Many horrifying examples of the blackmail of homosexuals are provided and good advice given to potential victims. The author calls male homosexuals 'Uranians', lesbians 'Uraniads', and prints as an appendix what must be one of the earliest self-analysis questionnaires on sexual subjects: 'A Categoric Personal Analysis for the Reader—"Am I at all an Uranian?"—"Am I at all an Uraniad?" ' Questions include: 'When came to you your first bodily proof of the *potency* of your genital system?', 'What would you say to be your chief *moral* weakness?', 'Do you instinctively use strong exclamations?', and 'Can you readily separate the great toe from its fellows by its *own* force?' Both these books are long overdue for transfer from the private case.

So is a pamphlet which, together with the newspaper cuttings mounted in it, is one of the essential sources for a future social history of homosexuality in this country: *The Phœnix of Sodom, or the Vere Street coterie* (1813), by one Holloway, who spent eighteen months in Newgate for a libel in it. He wrote it as a defence of James Cook, landlord of the White Swan public house in Vere Street, a meeting-place of male homosexuals. The White Swan had been raided by the constables in 1810 and twenty-three men arrested. *The Phœnix of Sodom* describes the furnishings of the house and the behaviour of those who frequented it:

Four beds were provided in one room: another was fitted up for a ladies' dressing-room, with a toilette, and every appendage of rouge, &c. &c.—a third room was called the Chaple [*sic*], where marriages took place, sometimes between a *female grenadier*, six feet high, and a petit maitre not more than half the altitude of his beloved wife! These marriages were solemnized with all the mockery of *bride maids* and *bride men*; and the nuptials were frequently consummated by two, three, or four couple [*sic*], in the same room, and in the sight of each other! . . . Men of rank, and respectable situations in life, might be seen wallowing either in or on the beds with wretches of the lowest description. . . .

It seems the greater part of these reptiles assume feigned names, though not very appropriate to their calling in life: for instance, Kitty Cambric is a Coal Merchant; Miss Selina, a Runner at a Police office; Black-eyed Leonora, a Drummer; Pretty Harriet, a Butcher; Lady Godina, a Waiter; the Duchess of Gloucester, a gentleman's servant; Duchess of Devonshire, a Blacksmith; and Miss Sweet Lips, a Country Grocer.

Still more instructive are the accounts of the treatment the accused men received at the hands of the London mob, largely a female mob, when they were put in the pillory. The crowds pelted them with mud, rotten eggs, offal and dung from slaughter-houses, vegetables, stinking fish, and 'the remains of divers dogs and cats', until they looked like 'bears dipped in a stagnant pool':

Before they reached half way to the scene of their exposure, they were not discernable as human beings. . . . The landlord of the house, a fellow of a stout bulky figure, . . . could not stow himself away as easily as the others. . . . Dead cats and dogs, offal, potatoes, turnips, &c. rebounded from him on every side . . . and nothing but the motion of the cart prevented him from being killed on the spot. . . . Before any of them reached the place of punishment, their figures were completely disfigured by blows and mud. . . . Upwards of 50 women were permitted to stand in the ring, who assailed them incessantly with mud, dead cats, rotten eggs, potatoes, and buckets filled with blood, offal, and dung. . . . On their return, a coachman stood upon his box, and gave Cook five or six cuts with his whip.

It is impossible for language to convey an adequate idea of the universal expressions of execration, which accompanied the monsters on their journey. . . . They were chained, and placed in such a manner that they could not lie down in the cart, and could only hide and shelter their heads from the storm by stooping. . . . Some of them were cut in the head with brickbats, and bled profusely.

That is how homosexuals were treated a century and a half ago. But compare the scene in 'Angela Pearson' (i.e. Diane Bataille), *The Whipping Club* (Paris, 1958), where— as in 'Peter Jason', *Wayward* (Paris, 1961)—'pansies' are introduced as an entertainment. After they have danced before debauchees, 'their athletic ballet-trained bodies beautiful in their nakedness', while 'many of the women gazed hungrily at them, and shook their heads sadly at the waste', they are flogged and one lady shows her appreciation of their beauty and their dancing by hissing: 'Scream! You bloody little queen! Scream! Oh Christ! I wish I could kill you!'

It is a relief to turn to *L'Alcibiade fanciullo a scola* (Venice, 1651), the first modern classic of homosexual love, a gem of erotic literature. The BM has the very early Oranges, 1652 edition; another in Italian; and three in French. Falsely ascribed to Aretino on the title-page, and long attributed to Ferrante Pallavicino (1618–44), who was executed for writing an attack on the pope, it is now known to have been written by Antonio Rocco, a Venetian professor of philosophy. It is a graceful description of the beauty of boys and the pleasures they offer, and of a boy's sexual education. I do not know of any English translation.

The first English erotic work dealing mainly with homosexuality is *The Sins of the Cities of the Plain or the recollections of a Mary-Ann* (1881), of which the private case

has a reprint, *c.* 1900. This is the life story of a male prostitute, who finds out by degrees that 'it is not so agreeable to
spend half-an-hour with a housemaid, when one has been
caressed all night by a nobleman'. The Boulton and Park
case, a notorious transvestite scandal of 1870, is alluded to,
and both Boulton and Park figure as characters in this book
and its rather less convincing sequel, *Letters from Laura
and Eveline giving an account of their mock-marriage,
wedding trip etc.* (1883), of which the private case has the
1903 reprint.

Suppressed Scenes from the Memoirs of Fanny Hill [*c.*
1901] is a greatly expanded version of the famous homosexual encounter in Cleland's novel. It is a clever pastiche
but flawed, as Dawes pointed out, by its 'somewhat late-
Victorian air':

> Take time, my dear boy, don't be in a hurry. This
> is too splendid for us not to make the most of it. Ah!
> you little rogue, how can I ever thank you for the ex-
> quisite pleasure you are giving me. There! there! that
> is just the way. Ah! you rogue, you are getting wild,
> too. Well, I suppose you can contain yourself no longer.
> Oh! such a delicious wriggle, that was.

Late-Victorian purple passages mar the most pretentious
clandestine homosexual fantasy: *Teleny, or the reverse of
the medal: a physiological romance of to-day* ('Cosmopoli'
[i.e. Paris?], 1893), sometimes attributed in part to Oscar
Wilde. The pianist Réné Teleny, remarkably good-looking
and eccentric enough to wear white heliotrope at his button-
hole when camellias and gardenias are in fashion, has
eyes with such penetrating power that Camille Des Grieux,
who has never really cared for women, feels all the blood in
his veins set aglow. Teleny saves him from suicide and they

kiss: 'The very quintessence of love was in these kisses. All that was excellent in us—the essential part of our beings—kept rising and evaporating from our lips like the fumes of an ethereal, intoxicating, ambrosial fluid.' Teleny offers to die with Des Grieux, but ' "No," quoth I, "let us live.". . . "I love you!" he whispered, "I love you madly! I cannot live without you any longer". . . Could this burning, unquenchable fire that consumed our bodies be called lust?' Well, yes; and though 'the hand of Time had stopped', Teleny's hand on the phallus of Des Grieux is 'as soft as a child's, as expert as a whore's, as strong as a fencer's', while Teleny's kisses up and down his friend's back resemble 'a rain of rose-leaves falling from some full-blown flower'.

'Now,' says Teleny, 'let us go in the next room and see if we can find something to eat. . . . I cannot give you a banquet.' Nevertheless they find Cancale oysters, 'of an immense size', a dusty bottle of Sauterne; a *pâte de foie gras* highly scented with Perigord truffles; a partridge with paprika; a salad made out of a huge Piedmont truffle; a bottle of exquisite dry sherry; a dish of Seville oranges, bananas, and pineapples, flavoured with Maraschino and covered with sifted sugar; a bottle of sparkling champagne; tiny cups of fragrant and scalding Mocha coffee; and a bowl of arrak, curaçao, and whisky punch flavoured with many hot invigorating spices. One begins to wonder what appetites this book is really intended to arouse. The food, by the way, is served in 'dainty blue old Delft and Savona ware, for he had already heard of my hobby for old majolica'.

Des Grieux soon learns of other hobbies: the friends are invited to a 'symposium', or homosexual orgy, the participants in which 'all have our little hobbies'. Des Grieux asks Teleny what clothes he should wear and Teleny replies: 'None.' But Des Grieux feels shy, so Teleny says: 'Well, then, a tight-fitting cycling suit; it shews off the figure best.' The entertainment includes a 'Priapean fountain': chartreuse is poured out of a long-beaked silver ewer on a man's chest, trickles over his belly, and falls from his penis into the mouth of a man kneeling in front of him, and 'the three men were so handsome, the group so classic, that a photograph was taken of it by lime-light'. An enthusiastic Spahi proposes to have a bottle inserted in his rectum—'it would be worse than buggery, it would be bottlery'—and this is accomplished, causing 'a mixture of acute pain and intense lechery'. To everyone's distress, not least the Spahi's, the bottle breaks. Rather than display his lacerated anus in a hospital, he shoots himself: 'his courage was indeed worthy of a better cause'. In the end Teleny too commits suicide when found by Des Grieux embracing the latter's mother.

Of more recent homosexual fantasies, 'Robert Desmond', *Professional Charmer* (Paris, 1961) is not without merit—at any rate, it has something of a plot—while 'Brett Edward', *The Passion of Youth* (Paris, 1960) is terrifyingly violent.

Some quite serious and often moving homosexual verse will be found in the private case—J. M. Stuart-Young's *An Urning's Love* (1905), for instance; *Rondeaux of Boyhood* (1923) by 'A. Newman' (i.e. Herbert Moore Pim?); and *Men and Boys: an anthology* (New York, 1924). Less serious is the spoof-Persian *Scented Garden of Abdullah the Satirist of Shiraz* (1910), from the pen of that old faker 'Aleister' (i.e. Edward Alexander) Crowley, and not to be confused with the other, early fifteenth-century *Scented Garden*. All but about seven copies of Crowley's book—a shameless imitation of Sir Richard Burton's annotations on eastern sex life—are said to have been destroyed by his Majesty's Customs in 1924. Poems and prose poems in praise of boys have such lines as 'If I had ever been angry with thee, O luscious-buttocked tulip' and

> Ye cypress-breasted boys of birth,
> attend the coming of the gloom!
> Expose your breasts of jasmine, show
> your lily buttocks all abloom!

Female homosexuality is little represented in the private case. Of some value to the social historian is *The Additional Petition of Miss Mary-Ann Woods and Miss Jane Pirie* ([Edinburgh], 1811), a document concerning two unmarried ladies who kept a school at Drumsheugh, near Edinburgh, and brought an action for defamation against the titled grandmother of a former pupil. This young woman deposed that she had heard Miss Pirie say, 'O, do it darling', to which Miss Woods replied, 'Not tonight'. Nevertheless the bed shook and she heard a noise like 'putting one's finger into the neck of a wet bottle'. There is a lesbian episode in 'B. von Soda', *Abandon* (Paris, 1958), where a relationship between two women is described as 'one of consideration for the needs and comfort of the other'; while in *The Whipping Club* identical twins called Sally and Jane masturbate each other with their big toes, a practice I have not found frequently alluded to elsewhere. Assiduous inquiries have failed to establish the existence of a lesbian fantasy literature written by or for women, the lesbian episodes that occur in ordinary pornography being clearly intended to excite the high proportion of male readers which finds the idea of such relationships stimulating: consult, for instance, *The Bagnio Miscellany* (1892 reprint), which includes another educational dialogue between two girls, and 'Harriet Daimler' (i.e. Iris Owens), *Innocence* (Paris, 1957).

Those studying the type of sexual behaviour in which erotic excitement is associated with pain or humiliation are particularly well served by the private case. The Stuttgart, 1957 reprint of Dr Ernst Schertel's *Der Flagellantismus in Literatur und Bildnerei* contains in its twelve volumes many pathetic photographs of flagellation, self-flagellation, tying up, and the often associated practices of nates fetishism, leather fetishism, and transvestism. And as for fantasies in this mode, the majority of English hard-core pornographic writings includes at least one flagellation episode; while a considerable number of books is devoted primarily to this and similar activities. Pornography is regarded by some as distasteful in proportion as it emphasizes cruelty, and for that reason they would like to see sado-masochistic erotica banned and those describing 'normal' sexual activity freely available to adults. This is a point of view with which I have much sympathy; but, as a recent judicial pronouncement once again stressed, there is little evidence to suggest that people are induced to inflict pain on others as a result of something they have read. The infliction of pain on children, for instance, is too common a practice in this country for it to be attributed to the reading of sado-masochistic erotica. Indeed, it may possibly be the case that such books serve as a safety-valve for persons with anti-social tendencies of a sadistic kind, enabling them to satisfy in fantasy the urges which, if fulfilled in life, would get them locked up. Fantasy is untrammelled, and the erotic literature which appeals to the sado-masochistic tendency inevitably exaggerates the nature, scope, and severity of the

117

actions described, just as 'normal' erotica commonly go beyond the limits of the possible.

The influence of Sade on English pornography goes back several decades before the publication by Isidore Liseux in Paris of the bibliographically interesting first English translation of the original *Justine* (1791), under the title: *Opus Sadicum: a philosophical romance* (1889). A thoroughgoing imitation of Sade, *The Inutility of Virtue*, was published in 1830, and the private case has a reprint of *c*. 1890. It is 'the history of a young and beautiful lady, modest and virtuous, who . . . is first ravished by a robber, then becomes successively the victim of lust and sensuality; till, overpowered by debauchery, her passions become predominant, her mind remaining pure, while her body is contaminated'. To Swinburne and others we owe the famous *Whippingham Papers* (1888 [1887]), while Sade's influence is also evident in 'Margaret Anson' (i.e. James G. Bertram?), *The Merry Order of St. Bridget* ('York, 1857' [i.e. London, 1868]); *The Yellow Room or, Alice Darvell's subjection* ('London' [i.e. Brussels?], 1891) by 'M. le comte du Bouleau'; *The Birchen Bouquet* ('London, 1895' [i.e. Paris or Brussels? 1896?]); and the quite horrible *Experimental Lecture* ('1836' [1878–79]) by 'Colonel Spanker', of which the private case has only the French translation, *Conférence expérimentale par le colonel Cinglant* ('Londres, 1880' [i.e. Amsterdam, 1886]). Likewise it has only the French translation ('Londres', 1892) of *With Rod and Bum, or sport in the West-End of London* [*c*. 1890?] by 'Ophelia Cox'.

Through all these books there is little to hear but the swish of whips and the cries of victims, generally female; and very tedious it becomes. There are a few exceptions. An author of moderately readable flagellation fantasies was

Georges Joseph Grassal (1867–1905), who called himself 'Hugues Rebell', and whose *Memoirs of Dolly Morton: the story of a woman's part in the struggle to free the slaves* (Paris, 1899) gives an account of aspects of Negro slavery in America which usefully supplements the history books. The same author's *Frank and I* (1902) is not in the private case; but a German translation is. The following passage from *Frank und ich* (Berlin, 1912), selected at random, shows that flagellation fantasies are often as internationally comprehensible as concrete poetry:

'Oh-h-h, Mama—bitte—bitte—hör'—auf.' Swisch! 'O-h-h—liebe—Mama—'. Swisch! 'Ei—ei—ei—je —je—je—, oh-h-h—ich—will—schon—brav—sein.' Swisch! 'Ah-h-h, oh-h-h,—ich—will—nie—wieder—' Swisch! 'Oh-h-h, ah-h-h—nie—wieder—Lügen— sagen.' Swisch! 'Weh—weh—weh.' Swisch! Swisch! Swisch!

Sadopaideia ('Edimburg' [i.e. Paris], 1907) is ascribed to Swinburne by Dr Anthony Storr, on what authority I do not know. It is not unlikely, for the book is quite stylishly written. It tells how Cecil Prendergast, undergraduate of the University of Oxford, 'was led through the pleasant paths of masochism to the supreme joys of sadism'. His guide is the seductive Mrs Harcourt ('I have never known such an expert in the art of love'), one of whose greatest thrills comes from whipping her maid Juliette between the legs. Before long, Cecil is going 'smack-smack-smack' on Juliette's reddening bottom, as she shouts: 'Harder, harder!' At last she cries: 'Take all of me, darling, my master.' The trio gradually extend their circle of initiates, and at one point a yokel named Ben confesses: 'That be a new game to I, to be whipped while one be vucking, but it baint bad.'

A good many variants on these themes have come out of Paris since 1955, most of them singularly lacking in even the moderate amount of imagination displayed by Sade. 'Ruth Lesse', in *Lash* (Paris, 1962), is much concerned with the flagellation of genitals and introduces a new kind of condom: a cap 'four times the size of a man's knob', with bristles attached, designed to give 'the maximum biting pain'. *The Whipping Club*, already mentioned, is a would-be nightmare of a book, in which whips go *tsutck* as they bite into flesh and those who faint under them are roused with smelling salts and cries of 'Cissy!' At Buckley Manor, about an hour out of London, behind gates resembling those of a medieval fortress, and with windows blocked up because 'on a still night, screams can carry a long way', is a torture-chamber fitted with ropes, chains, pulleys, belts, handcuffs, manacles, gags, flogging blocks, a medieval rack, thirty hot-water bottles to burn people with, 'and other machines of devilish ingenuity'. Victims include Rodney Pearce, a 36-year-old Cambridge mathematics don. Cords are tied round scrota, and two men so tied have a tug of war; a former bomber pilot runs the gauntlet on hands and knees; hypodermic needles are thrust deep into buttocks; and blood is licked off weals and swallowed. After Hitler's concentration camps it is all pretty tame, really, and sex will keep breaking in—for, as one character remarks: 'What's the use of flagellation if it doesn't lead to a bit of poking too?'

Of somewhat more interest to the social historian, if not to the psychologist, are the periodical outbreaks of public discussion on how to beat hell out of children. The private case has several examples, from *Letters Addressed to the Editor of the Englishwoman's Domestic Magazine* (1871 [1870]), to five big parcels full of the duplicated material issued by Mr Eric Arthur Wildman and his late and un-lamented Corpun Educational Organisation and National Society for the Retention of Corporal Punishment in Schools.

So far we have examined fantasies written almost ex-clusively from the point of view of the sadist or the domi-nant partner. Surprisingly few English erotica have been written from the opposite point of view. The most impor-tant of these is *Gynecocracy: a narrative of the adventures and psychological experiences of Julian Robinson (after-wards viscount Ladywood) under petticoat rule, written by himself* (1893). The happily miserable hero of this three-volume work is subjected to numerous refinements of humi-liation at the hands of a squad of severe young women. He is dressed as a girl, tightly corseted, birched, kicked, locked up in a wicker cage, and has stinking water poured over him. A governess urinates in his mouth, saying trium-phantly as he coughs, spits, and splutters: 'There, how do you like that? I do enjoy pissing upon you above all things; it is the only thing you really seem to mind. It does take it out of you and punish you.' But Julian's tribu-lations have only begun. His ears are pierced for golden ear-rings. He is circumcised and stung with nettles. And, as 'Miss Julia', he goes to bed with 'Lord Alfred Ridlington'; after a certain amount of fumbling they discover that 'Miss Julia' is a man, 'Lord Alfred' a woman: ' "What business have *you* to wear trousers?" I asked. "How dare you wear petticoats?" she retorted.' This book has been attributed to Havelock Ellis, and certain episodes do correspond with what is known of Ellis's sexual tastes.

The Petticoat Dominant, or woman's revenge: the auto-biography of a young nobleman ('Paris and New-York' [i.e. Paris or Brussels?], 1898) by 'M. le comte du Bouleau' again, is offered as a 'pendant' to *Gynecocracy* and is in fact an imitation of it, down to: 'She ... lifted her petticoats and peaed [*sic*] in my face.' A later imitation, *Miss High-heels* (Paris, 1931), is 'the story of a rich but girlish young gentleman under the control of his pretty step-sister and her aunt: written by himself at his step-sister's order, with an account of his punishments, the dresses he was made to wear, his final subjection and his curious fate'. Dennis, transformed into 'Miss Denise', has glass boxes fixed on his hands and feet, filled with brown dust that turns out to be myriads of biting fleas. He is also made to hold in each hand 'a horrible fat, big, slimy worm'. The ritualistic, indeed theatrical, character of masochism is well revealed in all three of these books.

Finally, a work which presents masochism exclusively from the woman's point of view, and does so with such power that few can read it completely unmoved. It may indeed have been written by a woman, though we have no means of ascertaining the sex of 'Pauline Réage', who is rumoured to be a French diplomatist and his mistress. However that may be, *Histoire d'O* (Paris, 1954), an English translation of which by Sabine D'Estrée was recently published in New York, is the most haunting book in this whole sado-masochistic phantasmagoria. Its flavour stays in the mind, perhaps because it has something to suggest about human relationships which, whether one agrees with it or not, transcends the conventional vapid formulas of erotic fiction; perhaps because in it the fantasy of a woman's utter submission to her lover is worked out with merciless logic.

The name chosen for the woman symbolizes, not only the female sex organ, the 'O' of pleasure, and the 'O' of pain, but also the cipher she gratefully becomes. Only by erasing her own will and fulfilling that of her lover, only by abnegating her humanity and suffering eagerly whatever physical and mental pain he chooses to inflict, or causes or permits to be inflicted, can O achieve happiness—'happiness in bondage'. She is whipped by him, and by others in his presence and absence; chained up; held by him while another possesses her and she cries out as she never did for her lover. He strokes her with a hand 'moist with the wetness and smell' of another woman. An ebonite rod is inserted in her anus for eight days, to render it easier of access. Her lover hands her over to his English friend Sir Stephen, who savagely buggers her and makes her masturbate before him. She is whipped between the legs and branded on the buttocks, and a ring bearing her name, Sir Stephen's name, and a device of a crossed whip and riding-crop is fitted through one of her labia. Finally, her head covered in an owl mask, she becomes a mere object, a living statue.

And all this, just because it is so painful and humiliating, and most of all because her body is giving pleasure to her master and his surrogate without limit or restraint, makes O happier than she had ever imagined possible. After the words 'THE END' comes this note: 'There exists another ending to the story of O. Seeing herself about to be left by Sir Stephen, she preferred to die. To which he gave his consent.'

Fifty years ago, *Histoire d'O* would have been relegated to the domain of sexual pathology. Today we can look more honestly into the human heart, for we know there are tendencies towards, and fantasies of, both cruelty and submission in 'normal' people. To read *Histoire d'O* is to become more understanding about some of the bypaths that love may legitimately take. Even for readers who have already come to terms with these aspects of themselves, it has an hallucinatory effect. At one level it is an erotic daydream transfigured by literary skill—notably by obsessive detail, Henry James's 'solidity of specification'—into something approaching genius. At a deeper level it is an allegory, chilling in its implications, of the human alienation to which we cling.

IX

THE TRUSTEES GO 'MODERN'

IN MARCH 1963 Mr Simon Nowell-Smith, president of the Bibliographical Society, complained in *The Times Literary Supplement* of 'a backlog of uncompleted cataloguing' in the British Museum's department of manuscripts. Mr Richard Cobb, the historian, sprang to the BM's defence. He compared the national libraries of Britain and France and expressed amazement that anyone could find anything to criticize in the BM catalogue, which was the best in the world. Mr Cobb's amazement in turn excited the surprise of Mr Terence Deakin, at that time an Oxford under-graduate. He himself had found the BM catalogue grossly unsatisfactory. Among other defects, he called attention to the practice of suppressing the call-marks of all books in the private case. This caused a great deal of inconvenience.

'It is not for an official of the British Museum to try to arbitrate between Mr. Cobb and Mr. Deakin', wrote the principal keeper of printed books, Mr R. A. Wilson. After answering various other criticisms, he added: 'Whether the Private Case books should be entered in the General Catalogue or not is a matter of opinion. The labour of doing so would require resources of staff which the Museum does not at present possess.' To which Mr Deakin, the compiler of *Catalogi librorum eroticorum* (1964 [1965]),

retorted that he would gladly undertake the task himself:
'Since there is already a printed catalogue of the Private
Case now confined to the Principal Keeper's office, all that
appears to be necessary is the pasting of slips into the bound
volumes in the Reading Room.' This generous offer was
not taken up, and nobody was less surprised than Mr
Deakin.

About the same time as this correspondence, close students
of the catalogue became aware of a significant innovation:
the introduction of yet another 'restricted' pressmark: Cup.
1000 and Cup. 1001. Readers applying for such works were
told they must write to the principal keeper stating their
reasons. Here in fact was a kind of liberalized annexe to the
private case. Just what caused a book to be so classified
was not immediately clear: illustrated books on erotic art,
available to any bookshop customer with thirteen guineas
or so in his fist—e.g. the *Roma Amor* (Geneva, etc., 1961)
and *Eros Kalos* (Geneva, etc., 1962) of Jean Marcadé—
are at Cup. 1000; so is the 1964 John Calder edition of
The Naked Lunch by William Burroughs. It seemed to be a
repository for recently and legally published works which
the authorities did not wish to be easily consulted, but which
they could hardly keep out of the catalogue in the nineteen-
sixties without looking ridiculous. It was an uneasy compromise.

How the 'resources of staff' were miraculously assem-
bled in a matter of months, I have not been able to ascertain;
nevertheless a rumour began to circulate that the trustees
had at last decided to break with the tradition of the past
hundred years and authorize the entry of private case books
in the general catalogue. It was whispered that the director
himself had proposed this change, though not all his colleagues viewed it with enthusiasm. Nor did all the trustees,

126

one of whom warned his colleagues that they would 'turn the north library into a masturbating parlour'.

Month succeeded month, and no public announcement was made. But the rumours grew more definite. In August 1965 I wrote to the principal keeper asking if they were true. Yes, he replied, they were. But this class of book raised 'a number of difficult bibliographical problems'; therefore 'the entering of them in the General Catalogue must be a gradual process'. Mr Wilson is not given to exaggeration. The problems are fiendishly difficult; the process was not made less gradual by a prolonged industrial dispute which had brought the printing of catalogue entries to a standstill. In the mean time, I reflected, it would surely be both logical and in the spirit of the trustees' decision to allow serious inquirers to see the private case catalogue. So I wrote and asked if there was any objection to this; I also asked if the regulations governing readers' access to private case books were available for inspection. Mr Wilson made this reply:

> The practice that governs readers' access to private case books derives from instructions issued by the Trustees. These instructions are not available for inspection.
>
> The catalogue of private case books, in accordance with these instructions, is not available to readers. In saying this I hasten to assure you that I do not question that you (and other readers of private case books) are serious inquirers.

I now wrote to the *TLS* and to the *New Statesman*, which had published letters on the question several months before. I pointed out that the trustees' decision would remove the last reasonable ground for complaint as far as the private case was concerned—if the authorities would also take the logical step of giving readers access to the private case catalogue. I added that it was hard to see why, after the trustees had decided to help students in this field, administrators should be permitted to nullify that decision in practice.

It was, I dare say, unfortunate that the trustees' decision should have been announced in the press by a reader and not an official. It would not be a bad thing, perhaps, for the BM to have a public relations officer or, at least, a public relations consultant, whose advice would be never to keep interesting decisions secret. Moreover a PRO might have made a better job of a reply to my letter than the one signed by Mr N. F. Sharp, a keeper in the department of printed books. The BM authorities, it said,

> have for many years been troubled by the difficulty of adopting a 'modern'* policy with regard to these books, without running the risks, of which in the past they have had only too much experience, of making books of this kind generally available. It is doubtful whether serious students in these fields have been at any considerable disadvantage as a result of the former policy of not entering Private Case books in the General Catalogue, but other students whose requirements are only marginally concerned may well have been inconvenienced. This situation is now being remedied as fast as the availability of staff time allows. The entry of these books in the General Catalogue is being treated as a normal cataloguing process, books are submitted for bibliographical examination and catalogue headings are being checked. In the meantime, no hardship should be caused to genuine seekers after knowledge,

* Note the quotation marks.

for our Reading Room staff are always ready to help in any difficulty there may be in ascertaining whether any particular book is in the collections.

An illuminating gloss on this letter was provided soon after its publication by an official who explained to a reader that the trustees' decision had been forced on them by publishers' post-war victories over censors—above all the cases of *The Philanderer* and *Lady Chatterley's Lover* and the Obscene Publications Act of 1959—but that they had no intention of providing 'a subject index to pornography'. The private case catalogue would remain secret, even when only a score, a dozen, or even one work in it had yet to be entered in the general catalogue. By the same token, private case books would continue to be omitted from the five-yearly subject indexes. In short nobody was going to be provided with a ready-made list of titles; so far as the officials were concerned, there would still be a hard core of hard-on books, and whoever wanted to see one would still have to know its title, or its author's name or pseudonym, and have the wit, patience, experience, or serendipity to find it in the general catalogue under whatever recondite heading that particular 'difficult bibliographical problem' had finally gone to ground. This applied whoever the reader was and whatever his purpose.

Those of my readers who have not visited the BM will be interested to learn that there are about 1,300 large folio volumes of the general catalogue, with several hundred pages in each. It is clearly impossible to check through the whole of this catalogue once a month, or even once a year, in order to find out what relevant new entries have been transferred, or otherwise incorporated. The need therefore arose for me to construct my own checklist of private case books. Basing myself on the last sentence in the above extract from the letter signed by Mr Sharp, I presented myself one morning at the reading room inquiry desk with a handful of slips, each bearing the title of a book.

'I have about 5,000 of these titles', I said. 'Each of them presents me with a difficulty of the kind envisaged by Mr Sharp. Will you check them for me one at a time? ten at a time? or a hundred at a time? Or shall I bring you the whole 5,000 at once?'

The consternation produced by this request exceeded my expectations. I was at first supposed to be joking, or mischievous. At length, the superintendent of the reading room told me he could not provide me with the full-time services of a research assistant. He ruled that I might occupy twenty minutes of one person's time each day. But this was inadequate; in twenty minutes scarcely a dozen titles could be checked with the requisite care, whereas I myself, if given access to the private case catalogue, could deal with 200 titles a day, possibly more. The matter came to the notice of Mr Chaplin, then keeper in charge of public services, who admitted that if a reader chose to stand at the inquiry desk all day presenting one bibliographical slip after another, nothing could be done to stop him. He was heard to add that Fryer had made his point, and that his intempestive persistence was foolish. Foolish or not, the very real prospect of other readers' following suit, of a lengthening daily queue of inquirers swamping the inquiry desk with such inquiries, made a lot of people's flesh creep.

I did not lack volunteers. An interesting situation might have developed (if the Sharp letter meant what it said) had not the principal keeper offered a compromise. He told me that if I would submit thirty bibliographical slips a day, five days a week, he himself would check them in the private case catalogue and provide me with the pressmarks. I should not then need to stand accusingly at the inquiry desk, and the research assistants could get on with their work. I thought this a reasonable offer; and until his retirement this summer Mr Wilson more than kept his word, frequently supplying details and dates of editions hitherto unknown to me, and jotting down pressmarks of other works by an author where I had submitted only one title. These thirty slips a day, which often came back with precious information, meant that though I was still groping in the dark, the principal keeper had been good enough to light a candle.

But the light it threw was dim and fitful. There is a big difference between using your own eyes and depending on someone else consulting a basic reference book on your behalf. Censorship is still censorship, even when half-hearted. As Mr R. T. Oerton put it in a recent *New Statesman* letter:

> Those who are denied access to truth or reality are to that extent diminished. Censorship presupposes that there are some people who can be trusted with knowledge and others who cannot, and that the first group can be trusted not only with knowledge itself but also with the right to deny it to the second group.

The present official attitude to these questions at the BM is a compromise between treating readers as adults and treating them as children; between free inquiry and censorship; between 'modern' and ancient policies; between science and taboo. The authorities seem to think that their one concession, which at the present rate must take years to implement, will disarm criticism. They are greatly mistaken. The maintenance of a secret catalogue and the censoring of the subject indexes are no less a public scandal than before. The present practice is open to criticism on five counts.

First, the general air of suspicion and disapproval with which applicants for private case books are regarded, and the obstacles put in their path, compare unfavourably with the practice of more enlightened custodians of erotica and sexological works. The member of the London Library or of the Wellcome Historical Medical Library, for instance, is not made to feel he is begging a favour when he applies for a book which needs special protection. BM practice turns a statutory right into a personal privilege. Here is the relevant section of the duplicated document *Information for those Superintending in the Reading Room* (1966):

PRIVATE CASE BOOKS. Some books not in the General Catalogue may be in the Private Case. The Superintendent should consult the Private Case catalogue in the Placer's Office or in the Principal Keeper's Room. If the book is in the BM the reader should then be asked to make written application, giving his reasons, to the Principal Keeper.

When the Principal Keeper is not in the Department, he is represented by the Senior Keeper or the Departmental Duty Officer.

The Superintendent may not show the P.C. catalogue to a reader. The Superintendent will examine the reader's ticket to see that it is a long period one and current and note the fact together with its number on the application. Applications from holders of short period tickets cannot be entertained. It will probably take some time before all P.C. books are entered in the General Catalogue. Even when they are, they will still require written application to the Principal Keeper, etc.

Some ' "modern" policy'! If a proper watch is kept on the readers to see they do not scribble, mutilate, or steal—and this is all that matters—what need is there for these restrictions?

But—and this is my second criticism—is a proper watch kept on readers? The number of books missing from the private case suggests that it is not. In one of my letters to the principal keeper, I asked how many such books were missing. 'So far as I am aware', he replied, 'no private case books are missing.' Well, I have news for Mr Wilson's successor. Here is a partial list of English books stolen from the private case:

BOOK	DATE AT WHICH THEFT WAS RECORDED
Amours of the Kings of France [*c.* 1845]	Between 1950 and 1952
Anecdotes of Female Flagellants [*c.* 1865]	November 25, 1947
'Birch, R.' *Venus School Mistress* ('Birchopolis', 1917)	November 26, 1965
* 'Bouleau, M. le comte du.' *The Yellow Room.* ('London' [i.e. Brussels?], 1891)	1947
Chidley, W. J. *The Answer* (Melbourne, 1911)	October 22, 1937
† *Fashionable Lectures* [1872?]	October 22, 1937
* *Flossie: a Venus of fifteen* (1904)	1948
* [Perret, Paul.] *Tableaux vivants* ('Athens' [i.e. Sheffield?], 1889)	193–?
The Voluptuarian Museum ('Paris' [i.e. London, *c.* 1825])	November 1942

* Now replaced.   † There is another copy in the private case.

This list could be extended; but enough has been said to prove that, in spite of the secret catalogue, the examination of readers' tickets, the requests in writing to the principal keeper, the endorsement of applications, books do get spirited away. The solution is twofold. First, watch the readers. No honest reader can object to supervision when he has a valuable book in his hands. Secondly, take photocopies of all the irreplaceable books in the private case, and issue the originals only to readers engaged on strictly bibliographical enquiries, who need to measure, collate, examine watermarks, etc.

My third criticism is that the regulations have always been applied arbitrarily, and still are. Personal friends of officials have always been favoured, and still are. I know of two readers who come in and read what they like, though, as far as I know, they make no claim to be engaged on serious research. And why not? But away with the pretence that high motives and serious purpose are prerequisites. Moreover two bibliographers have been allowed, not only to see the private case catalogue, but to copy it. One was the late Alfred Rose, who worked on it about the year 1934. The other was Mr Gershon Legman, who spent a week or so transcribing it about the year 1954. And why not? But away with the pretence that such a privilege is never granted.

In the fourth place, the museum authorities request and receive co-operation from those whose work they hamper in the ways I have described. I am all too well aware how little knowledge I have managed to acquire in the field of erotic bibliography. But what little I do know is always at the disposal of fellow readers and BM officials and staff. Indeed, since the final refusal to let me see the private case catalogue, hardly a fortnight has gone by without some request for information from the latter. Most come from the inquiry desk staff, who not only send readers to me, but ask: 'Have we got such-and-such in the private case, do you happen to know?' This is very flattering; but it is they who have access to the secret catalogue, not I. Better still, two assistant keepers, bless their hearts, consult me on such matters, and one of them gave my name, as a possible source of information, to a gentleman who teaches at the London School of Economics. Best of all, the assistant keeper who has been recataloguing the entire private case has more than once consulted me on knotty points of authorship, etc., and has even asked me to provide him with a proof, before publication, of my forthcoming catalogue of the English books in the private case. It would be of great help to him, he said. Fine. But how do they reconcile to themselves their refusal to let me consult the private case catalogue with their willingness to pick my brains of such small knowledge, in a notoriously obscure field, as I have acquired scrap by scrap in the teeth of BM obstruction?

And fifthly, all this nonsense about maintaining the secret catalogue, censoring the subject indexes, insisting on written applications, and automatically rejecting applications from holders of short-period tickets, conflicts with the grandiose claims made by the BM and with the duty of officials to help readers. '*All** the books in the department (excluding newspapers, maps and music) are recorded in the *General Catalogue*', says the 1962 guide to public services, which I wrote about in the Introduction. But it isn't true. 'Readers seeking works on a particular subject, are catered for by the *Subject Index*. In this *all** books in the library published since the year 1880 are entered.' But it isn't true. 'The *full range** of books in the Department is accessible to *any** holder of a reader's ticket.' Again,

* My italics.

it isn't true. It used to be the duty of the reading-room superintendent to 'assist the Readers in their studies and researches'. To be sure, this formulation was quietly dropped from *Statutes and Rules for the British Museum* some time in the nineteenth century. But it is still the superintendent's duty, according to the latest (1932) recension of that pamphlet, to 'see that Readers be provided with the books and other publications which they may require'. Moreover

> it is to be considered as a general instruction to all members of the Staff that they conduct themselves as becomes persons of honour, integrity and liberality, in the conscientious discharge of the duties of their respective stations, and as persons who have the credit and utility of The British Museum at heart.

The suppression of books, the maintenance of a secret catalogue, the censoring of subject indexes, the discouragement of serious inquirers, the hindering of free inquiry into sexual questions, the whole fog of furtiveness that envelops the subject of erotica at the BM: what have these anachronisms to do with honour, integrity, or liberality? No doubt many of the buried books would strike many people as 'nauseous balderdash'. But it was Macaulay who, quoting from a book he described in those terms, told his readers: 'I have been forced to descend even lower, if possible, in search of materials.' No book is out of place in a national library. And a librarian's job is to bring readers and books together, not thrust barriers between them. The BM librarians are compelled by law to interpret their task in this sense, as the British Museum Act of 1963 makes clear. The sooner they realize this the better it will be for everybody. The better it will be, above all, for scholarship in fields where the use of erotica, so long restricted by taboos, has now become a valuable auxiliary.

Censors and bureaucrats do not care for light to be thrown on their activities. I will end this chapter with a small example of the good such light can do. Among the books bequeathed to the BM by H. S. Ashbee were his own copies of two of the three volumes of his great bibliography, annotated by him and extra-illustrated with portraits of his French publisher friends. As late as the spring of 1965, six and a half decades after Ashbee's death, the BM had not seen fit to put these two volumes even in the secret catalogue of private case works. They were suppressed as effectively as if they had been burned in 1914, along with those other Ashbee duplicates. I happened to hear of their existence. I asked about them, verbally. The first reaction was a blank, bland denial that the museum possessed any such thing. I asked again. This time, the denial was a shade less categorical. Two letters to the principal keeper went unanswered, which was most unlike him. Then, along the grapevine, came the information that these copies were locked up in the principal keeper's room. Not for the incumbent's personal use. But a principal keeper of long ago had thought it 'not at all necessary for readers to see these duplicates', and so they were never catalogued, despite their interest to anyone working on Ashbee. For sixty-five years they were suppressed, without even being recorded in the handlist of suppressed books, the subject of the next chapter. I wrote again to the principal keeper and told him I knew where they were. This time he replied that they had 'now been catalogued'. Today they are in the private case.

Appearances to the contrary, it gives me scant pleasure to be a thorn in the flesh of officials who have a great burden of work and a still greater burden of responsibility. But I cannot believe that those two Ashbee volumes would have been rescued from oblivion if I had not persisted in asking about them. In themselves, they are not of earth-shattering importance. It is the principle which matters. How much more uncatalogued material is hidden away?

X

SECRETS OF THE S.S.

IN OCTOBER 1915, after Japan had entered the first world war on the British side but before the USA had done likewise, an anti-Japanese book was published in Boston and New York by the Houghton Mifflin Company. It was called *The Fall of Tsingtau: with a study of Japan's ambitions in China.* Japan had taken advantage of the outbreak of war to seize the German-leased port of Tsingtao, in the north-east Chinese province of Shantung, and extend military control to other parts of the province, outside the German protectorate. Jefferson Jones, American author of *The Fall of Tsingtau,* gave an eyewitness account of the Japanese occupation, which he described as a violation of Chinese neutrality. 'Though England has joined in the European war because Germany had violated the neutrality of Belgium,' he wrote, 'the British Government . . . did not think it necessary . . . to protest . . . to her ally in China against the very thing that had seemingly so shocked her in Belgium.' And, twenty-five years before the fall of Singapore, he asked whether the time was coming when Germany would be in league with 'the land of the Rising Sun . . . to drive Great Britain from the Far East'.

Energetic steps were taken by Scotland Yard to prevent the distribution of this book in Britain, and even to prevent any citizen from reading a copy in the British Museum. That the BM authorities had acted as political censors, on the direct instruction of the police, was a closely guarded secret until January 1966, when, under the fifty-year rule, the minutes of the BM trustees' standing committee for 1915 at last became available to the public. In fact the minutes for April to December 1915 cannot yet be inspected directly, since they are in a volume which contains minutes for later years. But the secretary of the museum, Mr Bentley Bridgewater, kindly offered to have extracts from the last nine months of 1915 typed out for me. The entry in the index volume, 'Book withheld from public use', yielded the following extract from the minutes for December 11, 1915:

> Read a letter from the Criminal Investigation Department (Metropolitan Police), 13th November, calling attention to a book printed in America ('The Fall of Tsingtau') and suggesting that, in view of its hostile attitude towards the Allies, the book should not be made available to Readers till after the war. The Director stated that the book, which had been received under Copyright, had been withheld from public use accordingly. The Trustees approved.

The Fall of Tsingtau was suppressed for a comparatively short period. Among the hundreds of suppressed and therefore uncatalogued books in the locked cases known as the 'S.S.' are some which have been there for over sixty years. And at least one royal relic was locked up in a table-drawer in the keeper's study in 1847 and later found its way into a cupboard in the principal librarian's room, though the trustees, as we shall see, had paid £70 of public money for it.

The only suppressed book I have ever applied for, the libellous *Life of Charles Bradlaugh, M.P.* (1888) by Charles

140

R. Mackay (in collaboration with William Harral Johnson and William Stewart Ross, though they did not put their names to it) had never been deleted from the general catalogue, and my application slip came back marked 'mislaid'. When I asked if I could see this ancient libel, in 1964, as part of my research for a book on the pioneers of birth control, the trustees conceded that it was not really 'mislaid' and gave me permission to see it. There was a slip in it saying 'To be returned to Mr Pine-Coffin', and the official who put it in my hands asked me not to publicize the fact that I had seen a copy in the BM. Since it is no longer suppressed, I no longer consider myself bound by this condition.

For a long time I believed that the list of suppressed books was not available to members of the staff. But in the spring of 1965 I discovered that a copy of it was kept at the inquiry desk in the reading room, where it was consulted from time to time, on behalf of unusually persistent readers, of whom there were not many, by the amiable research assistants who work there. I asked if I might examine the list and was referred to the no less amiable superintendent of the reading room, who advised me to write to the principal keeper, which I did, receiving the following reply:

The Handlist of suppressed books is not normally made available to readers. It is at present undergoing revision—a rather slow process in view of the investigations that such a revision requires. I do not wish to say that I will not let you see it in any circumstances, but perhaps you would be good enough to give your reasons in a little more detail. I should emphasise that the books listed in it are, for the most part, those which were confidential at the time we received them or were later found to be libellous. Many of the first class are, of course, still confidential and whether the second class can be seen must depend on whether the victims of the libels are still alive.

In my reply I gave details of my researches and asked:

Has Mr Pine-Coffin got locked away, in whatever kind of box a bibliotaph uses, any more libels on long-dead birth controllers? Or other relevant works which in their day were suppressed for no doubt excellent reasons but might now reasonably be exhumed?... The list is said to include a number of erotic works suppressed in pre-lamination days because they were literally falling, or crumbling, to pieces, and suppression was the only way to preserve them, for archival purposes, for posterity. Posterity will undoubtedly be grateful to the British Museum for this prudence; but whose interests are served by concealing the very existence of these works from a serious researcher in the fields of censorship and erotica?

The principal keeper, after 'a careful review of our practice', came to the conclusion that

since the handlist of suppressed books is a tool for internal use I cannot permit a reader to have access to it. I am sorry if this appears illiberal but, as I said in the first place, most of the books in it were withdrawn because they were found to be libellous or were never made available to readers because they were confidential. Books in both classes may, at a later stage, no longer need to be withheld. Hence the need for periodical revision of the list.

I then asked the principal keeper a number of questions:

Q.—Were the regulations governing readers' access to uncatalogued books available for inspection?

A.—'There are no regulations as such covering readers' access to uncatalogued books, if by uncatalogued books you mean those belonging to the class known as suppressed books. Since readers do not have access to them at all, regulations are not called for.'

Q.—What about the other books on the handlist: those which were neither libellous nor confidential?

A.—'I cannot give you a more detailed summary of the contents of this class of book than I have already sent you.'

Q.—Could Mr Wilson tell me how many readers had in the past been allowed access to the handlist, and under what conditions and in what circumstances; and how many of them had been allowed to copy it?

A.—'To the best of my knowledge no readers have in the past been allowed access to the Handlist of Suppressed Books nor has any reader been allowed to copy it.'

I also gave the principal keeper the titles of a number of books I thought might be on the handlist. Could he confirm that they were? To this he replied: 'Since all the suppressed books are withheld from circulation, I cannot give details about particular items.'

Now, I myself had seen the suppressed *Life of Charles Bradlaugh* a matter of months before. And, a matter of weeks before, I had seen, two places away from me on the 'front bench' in the north library, an Indian historian—now a professor of diplomatic history at Simla university—working on a series of volumes with S.S. pressmarks. I told the principal keeper I could not understand his assertion that 'readers do not have access to them at all'. 'Do you mean', I asked, 'that when an S.S. book is put into a reader's hands it automatically ceases to be suppressed for as long as he is working on it?' He replied: 'The *Life of Charles Bradlaugh* is not now suppressed. I cannot identify the other case you refer to, but it is possible that it concerned official prints that can be seen only on certain conditions imposed by the depositor or controlling department.' This exception clearly made nonsense of the claim that S.S. books were *never* shown to readers.

I now discovered that, a few days after my request to consult it, the handlist of suppressed books had been silently removed from the inquiry desk in the reading room. Whereas up to the end of May 1965 I or anyone could have found out whether or not a particular book was in the S.S. merely by asking at the inquiry desk, this facility was now withdrawn. I asked the principal keeper why, and he replied: 'The Handlist of Suppressed Books was removed from the Reading Room for administrative reasons.'

Lastly, I asked the principal keeper whether it was not a fact that the late Sir Henry Thomas (1878–1952), principal keeper in 1946–47, had given a copy of the handlist to the American bibliographer Mr Gershon (originally, George Alexander) Legman, himself author of a suppressed book, *Oragenitalism: an encyclopaedic outline of oral technique in genital excitation*, part I, 'Cunnilinctus' ([New York], 1940), written under the anagrammatic pseudonym 'Roger-Maxe de La Glannège' and seized and destroyed by the US police on publication. The principal keeper replied: 'I know nothing of what Sir Henry Thomas is said to have done in 1946/47, nor can I trace any information on this subject.'

As a pendant to this correspondence, I quote, for the last time, from *Information for those Superintending in the Reading Room* (1966):

SUPPRESSED BOOKS. The so-called suppressed books comprise mainly those which have been withdrawn by the publishers or authors, those which have been the subject of a successful action for libel, and those which are confidential and are deposited on condition that they are not issued for a certain period. Since none of the books in these classes is available to readers in any circumstances, the handlist is also withheld from readers and readers may not be told whether a particular book is in the list.

A few days after this document was distributed to certain members of the staff, the Indian professor of diplomatic history was back in the north library, checking his references in his pile of S.S. volumes. He had been given permission to see them in the first place, he told me, thanks to an application on his behalf from St Antony's college, Oxford, of which he was a fellow. He admitted that there had been some difficulty in obtaining them a second time to check his references; but the magic name of St Antony had at length done the trick.

And now, what dreadful secrets lie hidden in the S.S.—so dreadful that not even the titles of the suppressed books may be revealed to scholars? Up to 1915, the minutes of the trustees' standing committee provide a tolerably complete guide to book suppression at the BM; and gaps before that year can be filled in, and a skeleton key constructed for the past fifty years, by judicious conjecture based on legal records. Many of the books I shall name are certainly in the S.S.; many are almost certainly there; the few titles that are pure guesswork on my part I have indicated as such. For a time I thought I was on the way to solving the problem in detection set by the S.S. But the keepers of these dangerous books were too clever for me. For a short time after the withdrawal of the handlist of suppressed books from the inquiry desk, I was able to learn much from the form of words used by the ladies—unfailingly truthful, logical, and concise—who work there. If I asked about a book I could not find in the general catalogue and they said, 'This book is not in the British Museum', I could be certain they were telling the truth. If however they said, 'We are not allowed to tell you', this was a sure sign the book was in the S.S. But the keepers soon became aware of this weakness in their defences, and discouraged the research assistants from consulting the handlist. 'Since readers can never see these books, there is no point in looking them up', they would say. Still, a few titles had already escaped, never to be recaptured.

The S.S. contains, first of all, a number of books suppressed by the courts for alleged obscenity. This category is rapidly dwindling, since the practice now is to classify new books of this kind in the private case; many of the old lags are being reprieved, and transferred to the private case or the general library, in the course of the present revision of the S.S. handlist. Thus the first open homosexual novel in English—worse still in war-time, a pacifist novel—*Despised & Rejected* [1918] by 'A. T. Fitzroy' (i.e. Rose Laure Allatini, afterwards Scott), formerly at S.S. a.87, has now been entered in the general catalogue. So has the pirated edition of *Here Lies John Penis* (Paris, [1932]) by Geoffrey Wladislas Vaile Potocki, count of Montalk, containing a rendering of the 'Chanson de la braguette' of Rabelais and a parody of some lines by Verlaine, together with original poems. Formerly at S.S. A.409, it is now in the private case. So has the *Ladies Directory*, no. '7'–'10' (i.e. 1–4) and

146

duplicated supplement [1959–60], whose publisher was imprisoned for nine months. Formerly at S.S. Cup. 12.c.2, it is now at Cup. 1001. English and American editions of *September in Quinze* (1952) by Vivian Connell, condemned in 1954 during Sir David Maxwell-Fyfe's anti-vice drive, were by a happy accident transferred from S.S. Cup. 9.c.13 and S.S. Cup. 9.c.14 to Cup. 1000 a few days after I asked about them.

This process of desuppression of 'obscene' works, in the limited sense that the titles go into the secret P.C. catalogue, is not a new thing. Edward Charles's *The Sexual Impulse* (1935), described in chapter IV, had the pressmark S.S. A.408, but was transferred to the private case in 1953 by Mr (now Sir) Frank Francis, then a keeper in the department of printed books. *Nell in Bridewell* [1934], a translation of W. Reinhard's flagellation novel *Lenchen im Zuchthause* (Karlsruhe, 1840), desuppressed about the same time and given a Cup. 364 pressmark, was stolen in 1959. A book seized by the police and destroyed, *The Autobiography of a Child* [1921], formerly pressmarked S.S. a.78, was recently desuppressed and placed at Cup. 1001. Two of Wildman's booklets on flagellation, *Modern Miss Delinquent* (1950) and *Punishment Posture for Girls* (1951), withdrawn on legal advice before publication, were for some years at S.S. Cup. 6.b.5 and S.S. Cup. 6.b.11 respectively, but are both now in the private case.

To the best of my knowledge, the following books are still in the S.S.: the first edition of *The Cantab* (1926) by Shane Leslie, prosecuted and destroyed after censure by the Roman Catholic bishops; *Sleeveless Errand* (1929) by Norah C. James, successfully prosecuted because one of the characters says, 'For Christ's sake give me a drink' and the words 'balls', 'bloody', and 'bugger' are printed;

147

Brass and Paint: a patriotic story (1934) by Terence Greenidge, author of *Degenerate Oxford?* (1930); William Henry Waldo Sabine's long poem *Guido and the Girls* (4th edn, Harrogate, 1934), in which Lord Halifax (1881–1959), former viceroy of India, is lampooned, and which cost its author a £500 fine for publishing an obscene libel (a copy is now in the private case); Wallace Smith's *Bessie Cotter* (1935), a novel about the life of a Chicago whore (the private case now has a copy of the 1938 reprint by the Obelisk Press in Paris); and *To Beg I Am Ashamed* (1938) by 'Sheila Cousins', a London whore's autobiography (two later editions are in the general catalogue).

Next, the S.S. contains a large number of books which have been the subject of successful libel actions. This has been a sore spot with the BM authorities ever since 1893–94, when the case of Martin et Uxor *v.* the Trustees of the British Museum and E. M. Thompson, though decided in the trustees' favour, showed that it was technically possible to 'publish' a libel by letting readers see defamatory books. In February 1893, John Biddulph Martin, husband of Victoria Claflin Woodhull (1838–1927)—the celebrated American feminist, broker, medium, and presidential candidate—wrote to the museum listing six works he wanted withdrawn from public use, on the ground that they libelled his wife, or contained obscenities about her. One of the books complained of, *The Sexual Problem*, could not be found in the museum; *The Beecher-Tilton Scandal* (published, I think, in Brooklyn, 1874) was 'sealed up as an obscene work'; two other books, against which Martin did not appear to have taken legal proceedings, remained in the general library; and expurgated editions of two more were, if possible, to be substituted for the editions complained of. Such were the trustees' decisions. They then formally adopted, on the suggestion of Richard Garnett, keeper of printed books, the rule that

> the genuine prosecution of legal proceedings should be the criterion of Museum action, except when the publication was *per se* condemnable; and that, in the event of such legal action being dropped, works withdrawn should be again made available, but that expurgated editions should be procured when issued in deference to judicial censure.

The trustees' decisions did not satisfy Martin and his wife, who threatened proceedings against the trustees and the principal librarian unless they revealed the name of the person who had sold *The Beecher-Tilton Scandal* to the BM,* aid in his prosecution, and publish in the daily papers an expression of their regret. The trustees refused. The principal librarian, Dr Edward Maunde Thompson (1840–1929) even suggested that the trustees threaten to close the reading room and newspaper room 'pending legislation by the government for their protection'. But the trustees, feeling perhaps that such militancy would not sway the courts in their favour, declined to adopt this suggestion.

The case was heard in February 1894 before Mr Baron Pollock and a special jury in the queen's bench division. Besides *The Beecher-Tilton Scandal*, the plaintiffs also complained of BM 'publication' of *The Story of Henry Ward Beecher and Theodore and Mrs. Tilton* (1874) by the editor of the *Anglo-American Times*. Mrs Martin, giving evidence, said she would not say her spiritual adviser was not Demosthenes and added, amid laughter: 'There is an apparition appearing to me now.' The jury found that the documents

* It was the Vermont bookseller and bibliographer Henry Stevens (1819–86).

complained of were libels on Mrs Martin; that the defendants bought the books in the belief that they were discharging their statutory powers and duties; that they neither knew nor ought to have known that these books contained libels; that they were not guilty of any negligence; but that they had not discharged their duties with proper care, caution, and judgment. The jury assessed damages, should the defendants be held liable in law for publishing the libel, at twenty shillings. A few days later, the judge found for the defendants, with costs of £508 13s. 8d.

The next meeting of the trustees' standing committee decided that *The Beecher-Tilton Scandal* must remain withdrawn from the catalogue and sealed up; to be on the safe side, copies of *Woodhull and Claflin's Weekly* for November 1872 and February 1873 were to be similarly dealt with; and the first edition of a biography of Beecher containing passages cancelled in subsequent editions was to be withdrawn. Although Mrs Martin died in 1927, all these are still in the S.S. The other works Martin had originally complained of were restored to public use. Garnett also recommended the withdrawal from the catalogue and library shelves of J. E. P. Doyle's *Plymouth Church and its Pastor* (Hartford, Conn., 1874), which contained matter attributed to Mrs Martin but disclaimed by her; and the trustees approved. This book, later pressmarked S.S. a.13, was desuppressed about thirteen years ago.

This legal action set a precedent which has been followed ever since.

The libellous *Life of Charles Bradlaugh* had not been suppressed by the trustees until 1892, the year after Bradlaugh's death, and not until the solicitors of his daughter and executor specially asked them to. The trustees then ordered 'that the Museum copy of the work . . . be withdrawn from the Library Catalogue, sealed, and kept in the Department of Printed Books'. By some oversight, the catalogue entry was not in fact deleted, or 'excorporated', as the cataloguing staff call it. So much has already been said. Nor was it yet, apparently, the practice to give such works an S.S. pressmark; this practice started, and the S.S. handlist was compiled, some time in the twenties—perhaps because a greater number of confidential official documents was deposited at the BM during the first world war. Even then, for some reason, the *Life of Charles Bradlaugh* was not given an S.S. pressmark.

In 1893 the libellous first edition of Major Henri Le Caron's *Twenty-five Years in the Secret Service* (1892), against which proceedings had been taken by an ex-M.P. named Kelly, was ordered to be sealed up; the general library has the expurgated sixth edition. Mamie Bowles's libellous novel *Charlotte Leyland* was suppressed in 1900, having been withdrawn from circulation by its publisher, Grant Richards; the trustees ordered that it be 'removed from the Library shelves and kept under lock and key in the Department'. In the following year, Jessie Bedford's *The Harp of Life*, from the same publisher, was withdrawn from the catalogue and locked up for the same reason. By 1912 the trustees' minutes are referring to 'the locked case reserved for such books', which shows they had already outgrown the table-drawer in the keeper's study. The phrase quoted was used in an entry recording the trustees' refusal, on the ground that the book had been stamped, to return to Mr T. Werner Laurie, publisher, an unnamed book 'delivered by him under the Copyright Act, and now withdrawn from circulation as containing libellous matter'.*

* It was probably *Woman and Crime*, by Hargrave Lee Adam, issued in a modified form in 1914.

Among more recent libels, the S.S. includes: *Anna Craft* (1936) by Richard Ford, a first novel in which the *Times Literary Supplement* reviewer found 'considerable insight and sincerity', but which libelled a prominent woman journalist; *Coronation Commentary* (1937) by Geoffrey Dennis, a book suppressed not because of its anti-semitism but because it libelled the duke of Windsor; *Dinner at the White House* (1946) by Louis Adamic (1899–1951), which libelled Churchill by alleging that he had been on the verge of bankruptcy in 1912; and the first edition of Constantine Fitz Gibbon's *When the Kissing Had to Stop* (1960), withdrawn from circulation in 1961 because it libelled a night club proprietor. Though this last work is in the S.S., there is still an entry for it in the general catalogue, and one's application slip comes back marked 'mislaid'.

An alternative to outright suppression, much used at the turn of the century, was the substitution of reprinted pages for those containing defamatory matter. Thus, in 1900, the trustees approved such a substitution in Joseph Bell's *Notes on Surgery for Nurses* (5th edn, 1899), a nurse having considered herself libelled by a reference to 'fast women' masquerading in nurse's uniform. In the same year a fresh page was substituted, in Georg Schweitzer's *Emin Pasha: his life and work* (1898), for a page libelling a *New York Herald* correspondent named Vizetelly; the offending page in the BM copy of the German original, *Emin Pascha* (Berlin, 1898) was simply removed and no substitute inserted. In 1904 the trustees ordered that a libel on page 101 of volume I of Charles Booth's *Life and Labour of the People in London* be obliterated; if this was done, no trace of the obliteration remains.

Breach of copyright is another reason for burying a book in the S.S., and Alice Corkran's *Miniatures* (1903) is there for that reason. Errors of fact, if they are serious enough, may cause suppression. The S.S. has a copy of Colonel Sir Henry Knollys's *Life of General Sir Hope Grant* (1894), in which the double crime of having borrowed £100 from a bank manager in his youth and having, in later life, saved the same bank by depositing £30,000 is wrongly attributed to a Mr Levi or Levy of the *Daily Telegraph*. In 1898 the trustees ordered that this naughty book be 'withdrawn and sealed up', rejecting the alternative suggestion of the insertion of a printed slip. The joke is that another set of the same work, with the erratum slip, was presented to the BM in 1920 by Major J. H. Leslie of the Royal Artillery and was duly catalogued.

Then there are strange publications containing commercial secrets, produced confidentially for subscribers only but deposited at the BM under the Copyright Act. These all go into the S.S. and are therefore uncatalogued and unread. There is, for instance, an annual called *Credit Index*, which began publication in 1893 and is still, for all I know, confidentially indexing credit. A similar periodical, *Seyd's Commercial List*, was going strong in the same year, when Messrs Kelly & Co. Ltd unsuccessfully sought the trustees' permission to consult it.

Another reason for putting a publication in the S.S. is that it contains official or police secrets. A periodical called *The Police Journal* is in the S.S., from its first issue in 1928 onwards, though it was not restricted to members of the police force until 1936. Whoever wishes to consult the issues for 1928–35 has to visit Manchester public library or the Bodleian. I have it on good authority that a number of books containing information on lock-picking and safe-breaking are in the handlist of suppressed books, perhaps because Scotland Yard has asked for them to be withheld from readers. The apprentice burglars, train robbers, and political assassins who throng the reading room are also forbidden to read up-to-date books on explosives, which have been suppressed since 1894. In that year the Home Office asked the trustees to withhold from readers a proposed new edition (1895) of the late Lieutenant-Colonel John Ponsonby Cundill's *Dictionary of Explosives*, and suggested that the chief inspector of explosives should vet any applicant for it whose bona fides were not unimpeachable. The trustees agreed that no entry of the book should appear in the catalogue, that it be kept under lock and key, and that nobody have access to it without the keeper's express permission. All similar books received since 1880 were removed from the shelves in 1906, and the trustees reaffirmed their attitude to such books in 1917.

Two books revealing naval secrets may be in the S.S.; I suspect they are, but cannot be certain. One is called *Statement respecting the Prevalence of Certain Immoral Practices in his Majesty's Navy* (1821); the other is Lieutenant (afterwards Captain) Alfred C. Dewar's *On Certain Naval Matters* (Edinburgh, 1908). That military secrets— if there are any left—get into the S.S. from time to time is suggested by an entry in the trustees' minutes for June 11, 1910. A letter had been received from the War Office about some military plans included in the library of king George III and sealed up in 1837 at the request of the Board of Ordinance. There was no longer any need for such precautions, said the letter; so the trustees ordered that the plans be unsealed and made available in the usual way.

Political censorship does not seem to have been confined to *The Fall of Tsingtau*. In 1904 the trustees suppressed, ostensibly as libellous, a book called *The Truth about the Civilisation in Congoland* (1903) by 'a Belgian'; they also

154

suppressed, proleptically ('if received, to be locked up and withheld from the use of Readers') another criticism of Belgian administration of the Congo Free State, as it then was: *The Curse of Central Africa* (1903) by Guy Burrows. *The Indian Sociologist* (1905–22), a monthly published in London and received at the BM under copyright, is in the S.S. It was suppressed—'removed from general circulation' —in 1907, when the trustees were informed that, according to a printed heading to the October issue, it had been prohibited in India by the British government. Seven volumes of the Curzon papers—the weekly reports written by Lord Curzon of Kedleston (1859–1925) while viceroy of India from 1898 to 1905—are in the handlist of suppressed books (pressmark S.S. Cup. 7.a.1), together with about twenty-five volumes of additional correspondence by Curzon relating to India. These prints, despite the claim that suppressed books are in no circumstances shown to readers, have been seen within the past two years by two research workers whose names are known to me. I understand that other printed collections of documents by viceroys of India are in the S.S., too, and that it is not insuperably difficult to persuade the trustees to let one see them, though inquirers are told initially, as a matter of form, to 'try the India Office library'.

Books saying unseemly things about the holy family, or making disloyal revelations about the royal one, are in the S.S. A famous 'blasphemous' publication apparently kept there is the Christmas 1882 number of *The Freethinker*, with would-be comic sketches of the life of Christ, modelled on, or reproduced from, *La Bible amusante* (Paris, 1881–82) and *La Vie de Jésus* (Paris, 1882) by 'Léo Taxil' (i.e. Gabriel Antoine Jogand-Pagès), copies of which are in the private case. For this issue of *The Freethinker* its editor

George William Foote (1850–1915) was sentenced to twelve months' hard labour. Also in the S.S. may be a copy of *Rib Ticklers, or questions for parsons*, published by John William Gott and suppressed in 1911. I rather suspect that some of the pamphlets in which queen Victoria was disrespectfully referred to as 'Mrs John Brown' or 'the Empress Brown' might be found in the handlist; I gather that those who have investigated the question have been told by officials that the library possesses nothing of the kind. I should also like to see whether *The Peer in the Bookseller's Shop, or the cuckold of royalty* (1820) by 'Roger Hunter' is in the handlist. What the S.S. certainly does have is a copy of *The Modern Characters from Shakespear* (1778) with manuscript notes by king George III. This was acquired in 1847 and has been locked up ever since. It seems to have been the first book the BM suppressed. The trustees' minutes for July 10, 1847 record that

> Mr. Panizzi submitted to the Trustees a letter from Mr. [afterwards Sir Thomas] Baylis offering at the price of £70 a copy of *The Modern Characters of Shakspere* with Manuscript notes by George III. The Trustees inspected the volume. The Trustees directed the volume to be purchased; and Mr. Panizzi to keep it in his own charge, and not to allow any extract to be made from it without the special permission of the Trustees.

In March 1891 this book was reported missing, and the trustees ordered a search to be made. A retired official recollected it as having been kept in a table-drawer in the keeper's study. Eight years later, the director found it in a cupboard in his official room and reported accordingly to the trustees. The book, he told them, had been successively in the custody of Sir Anthony Panizzi, Mr Winter Jones, and Sir Edward Bond. The trustees ordered 'that the book be kept locked up in charge of the Keeper of Printed Books'. And there it remains to this day, unknown to historians and to George III's many biographers. £70 was a lot of money for a book in 1847; whatever can there be in those manuscript notes?

Other distinguished families receive similar protection on occasion. *Contemporary Account of the Separation of Lord and Lady Byron* (privately printed, 1870) by John Cam Hobhouse, baron Broughton (1786–1869) is in the S.S., the trustees having decided in 1896 that a copy bought at a public sale be sealed up until 1900, and in 1900 that it be locked up indefinitely. Another copy was bought in 1937, however, and is in the general catalogue.

One final category of S.S. books is, I believe, very small; and I hope the present book does not swell it. I refer to criticisms of the administration of the British Museum. I must admit that those who have ventured such criticisms have rarely covered themselves with glory. One of them, an eccentric Polish refugee named Stefan (or Stephan) Poles, sold his scurrilous pamphlet, *The Actual Condition of the British Museum* (1875), at the museum gates and died in poverty a few months later, friendless and 'raving in an unknown tongue'. His pamphlet contained so much personal abuse of the BM officials that the trustees ordered it to be 'withdrawn from the Reading Room'. A copy with manuscript notes by Garnett was bought in 1959 and entered in the catalogue, and I gather that another copy remains in the S.S.

In the letter printed above the name of Mr N. F. Sharp in the *TLS* for October 21, 1965, from which I quoted in chapter IX, the following defence was attempted of the BM attitude to suppressed books:

> The 'suppressed books'* . . . consist of the following: those which have been pronounced libellous by a court, those which have been found to infringe copyright, and those which are at the time of deposit confidential. There are also certain other books which were originally presented to the Museum on condition that their presence in its library should not for a period of time be revealed. The Trustees are pursuing a policy of derestriction of suppressed material wherever possible, but the examination of the records concerned, which are often difficult to trace, is necessarily a laborious process.
>
> The list of suppressed books which Mr. Fryer complains has been unjustifiably removed from the Reading Room was available to the Reading Room Staff in the first place to help readers with their enquiries, but after a time it was found to lead to requests which could not, because of insufficient evidence about the reasons for a book's 'suppression',* be met.

The second of these two paragraphs must be one of the most extraordinary declarations ever to come out of a British institution. For it contains two quite damaging admissions. First, the officials admit they simply do not know why some, at least, of the suppressed books were ever suppressed in the first place—and yet, in spite of the 'insufficient evidence', they persist in denying to scholars even the titles of such books. Secondly, they admit their policy on this question is governed by a desire to reduce the bother

* Note the quotation marks.

caused by the very few readers who occupy themselves with such matters. The 'administrative reason' why the S.S. handlist was removed from the reading room turns out to be that—it led to embarrassing requests. In removing the handlist, the authorities reverted to their time-honoured attitude of saying as little as possible about these things and hoping that awkward readers will go elsewhere, give up in despair, or die. This attitude is indefensible in principle and inexpedient in practice.

I am not demanding that libellous books should be freely available at the BM. It is not inconsistent with literary and scholarly freedom, but rather a condition of such freedom, that a libel be restricted during the lifetime of the person libelled. About official 'secrets' I am not so sure, partly because many of them are open secrets whose continued suppression is mere governmental face-saving. Here is a case in point. Like many other readers, I take pride in being able to help the BM from time to time by presenting books and microfilms; but when, some months ago, I was approached by an official who asked if I could get hold of a copy of the 'Spies for Peace' document (1963), which for obvious reasons they had not obtained under copyright and had not been able to acquire from an official's daughter who was an active CND supporter, I asked: 'Will you put it in the S.S.?' The reply was: 'Yes, in all probability.' Regretfully, I did not find myself able to co-operate. Thousands of people have copies of this document; for the BM to keep it out of the catalogue would be an absurd piece of political censorship. If they feel that way, they had better do without it.

In any case, it is hard to see how the interests of victims of libels, or of officialdom, or of anyone else, would be harmed in the slightest merely by readers being given access to the

S.S. handlist. It is high time the museum authorities realized that the uncatalogued books in their care are not their private property, and that their refusal to let people know exactly what they have and have not got is unworthy of a great national library and totally inimical to scholarship.

The BM authorities will not budge unless public opinion forces them to. As long as we let them, they will clog scholarship and free inquiry by maintaining this curious pocket of censorship. Liberalization will continue only to the extent that opponents of censorship press for it. The first essential is to make it known how censorship at the BM operates. That is why I have written this book.